Cambridge Latin Course

Book II

dent Study Book

FOURTH EDITION

CAMBRIDGE
UNIVERSITY PRESS

CAMBRIDGE UNIVERSITY PRESS

Cambridge, New York, Melbourne, Madrid, Cape Town, Singapore, São Paulo

Cambridge University Press
The Edinburgh Building, Cambridge CB2 8RU, UK

www.cambridge.org
Information on this title: www.cambridge.org/9780521685931

© University of Cambridge School Classics Project 1997, 2001, 2007

First published by the University of Cambridge School Classics Project
as *Independent Learning Manual Book II* 1997
Second edition 2001
Fourth edition 2007

Printed in the United Kingdom at the University Press, Cambridge

A catalogue record for this publication is available from the British Library

ISBN 978-0-521-68593-1 paperback

Preface

This *Student Study Book* is designed to be used in conjunction with Book II of the *Cambridge Latin Course* (ISBN 978-0-521-64468-6). It is intended for use by students in the following situations:

- students learning Latin on their own

- students on short courses who have to do much of the work on their own

- students being taught privately and requiring additional support material

- students who are catching up after illness or a change of schools

- students working ahead of the rest of the group

- teachers who wish to set cover work for a class

- classes in which independent learning is encouraged

- classes containing groups of students working at different levels.

An Answer Key is also available (ISBN 978-0-521-68594-8), as are online resources and e-tutor support (see page v).

The *Student Study Books* are re-workings of the earlier *Independent Learning Manuals*. In the creation of the original materials we benefited greatly from the advice and help of many teachers and students. In particular we should like to thank the following: Julien Melville for generously allowing us to make use of his own materials; Richard Woff, Neil Williams, Eileen Emmett, Betty Munday, Alex Nightingale and Wilf O'Neill for reading the draft materials and making many helpful suggestions and criticisms; Helen Vicat, whose ideas for pictures and skill in executing them have enlivened several pages; Helen Forte for her talented and witty artwork; Jean Groombridge; Christine Spillane; Joan Wootten; Jill Dalladay, for her suggestions for comprehension questions and exercises; Roger Dalladay, for his notes on the illustrations; Christine Simister, who pioneered the use of independent learning materials with the *Cambridge Latin Course*.

We are grateful to the following teachers and students who trialled the materials: Lucy Harrow and students at St Teresa's School, Dorking; Neil Williams' students at South Park Sixth Form College, Middlesbrough; David Karsten and students at Ranelagh School, Bracknell; Marian Small and students at St Margaret's School, Bushey; Jean Hubbard and her students at Banbury Community Education Council and Pat Story and her students at Coleridge Community College, Cambridge.

Finally, we should like to thank Betty Munday and Margaret Widdess for much detailed and demanding work; Debbie James for her meticulous reading of the texts; Maire Collins for designing and setting the original texts with such patience, care and ingenuity; and Jean Hubbard and Pat Story for all their work in developing, creating and editing the original *Independent Learning Manuals*. To these and all our other helpers we are much indebted.

Cambridge School Classics Project

July 2006

Introduction

Welcome to Book II of the *Cambridge Latin Course*. We hope you will enjoy learning more Latin and finding out about the lives of people in two very different parts of the Roman Empire. Stages 13–16 are set in Roman Britain, Stages 17–20 in Alexandria in Egypt.

What you need to begin

The *Cambridge Latin Course Book II*, Fourth Edition.

If possible, you should have the *Cambridge Latin Course Worksheet Masters for Book II*. This is a pack of photocopiable additional exercises on language points, word derivations and the cultural background sections.

If you do not have a teacher to mark your work, you will need the *Student Study Book II: Answer Key*.

These books are obtainable from Cambridge University Press.

Online resources

All the stories in *Cambridge Latin Course Book II* are available online in 'exploring' format. This allows you to click any word and see the vocabulary definition for that word instantly. You will also find interactive comprehensions, activities for practising grammar and many carefully selected weblinks for each Stage of the book. All the resources are available free of charge at www.CambridgeSCP.com.

E-tutor support

If you would like tutored support through the book, we can provide you with a distance e-tutor and study guide. You may begin your course whenever you choose and study at whatever pace suits you – your tutor will be on hand to help you for up to 40 weeks. All you need is a computer with an internet connection and an email account. For more information, please visit www.CambridgeSCP.com.

How to use this Student Study Book

If you turn to page 1, you will find instructions for working through Stage 13. This book has the same headings as those in the textbook. It also gives page references to the textbook, e.g. **Model sentences** pp. 2–4. Start working through the material in the order given in this book which is sometimes different from that in the textbook. This is to give you more variety.

You may wish to use an exercise book for your answers. Although there is space in this book for some shorter answers, there is not space for answers to every exercise.

How to check your answers

Check

This sign tells you when to check your answers. You do this by using the separate *Answer Key* if you do not have a teacher to help you.

When you are checking the translation of a story, you may find that you have used different expressions from those in the *Answer Key*. If their meaning is the same, your translation will be correct. In order to help students, the *Answer Key* often gives a rather literal translation and you may be able to think of better, more idiomatic expressions.

How to learn efficiently

It is better to have several short sessions a week than one or two long ones. If you have only one or two long sessions in school or college, try to find short periods of time (even 10 minutes) in between to revise what you have learnt. This is particularly important when learning vocabulary or grammar.

Use active learning methods whenever possible; for example, in learning vocabulary, learn a few words and their meanings; then cover up the English meanings and give yourself a mini-test; better still, ask someone to test you. Then learn the next batch and give yourself another test.

How to keep track of your progress

You will find a **Progress record** at the end of each Stage in this book. You can use it to record work as you do it or to note any questions you would like to ask your teacher. Use the Revision section for any particular points from the whole Stage which you need to continue to revise.

How to pronounce Latin

The best way to learn to pronounce Latin is to listen to a teacher reading from the textbook and then imitate him or her.

Both in the textbook and in this book you will see that many Latin words have marks over some of the vowels. This is to help you to remember that those vowels have a long sound; e.g. **ā** in **māter** is pronounced like the *a* in *father*.

There is a **Short guide to the pronunciation of Latin** on p. 98.

Stage 13 in Britanniā

In Stage 13 you are transported to Roman Britain in AD 82. The Romans have been in Britain for nearly forty years, but are still fighting the tribes in the north. The south, where our stories are set, is peaceful: the towns are flourishing but most of the population live in the countryside and continue to farm as they have always done. Some of the wealthier farmers begin to rebuild their farmhouses in the Roman style.

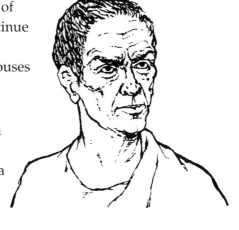

The man in the picture is Salvius, an important Roman administrator. He appears in this Stage with his wife Rufilla and several of his slaves. He is then seen at work, inspecting a Roman mine, where he escapes an attempt on his life. He finally returns to his large country estate to check that it is being run efficiently.

Picture p. 1

This shows a reconstruction of a British farmhouse. What differences are there between this and the Pompeian town houses you are familiar with from Book I? How different is the appearance of the farmer and his wife from that of Caecilius and Metella? To find out more about the Britons and their farms, turn to pp. 16–17 and read the information.

Check

Model sentences pp. 2–4

The setting for these is Salvius' large country estate where he lives in an elegant Roman villa.

p. 2 Here are the people in authority on Salvius' estate. Work out the meaning of sentences 1–3. The new words are in the box below.

vīlicus	*farm manager, bailiff*
cūrat	*looks after, supervises*

pp. 3–4 Here are some of Salvius' slaves. Read sentences 4–9 and see if you can answer the questions below.

fessus	*tired*
vōcem	*voice*
suāvem	*sweet*
agilis	*agile*
saltāre	*dance*
geminī	*twins*

Sentences 4 What is Philus holding? How does it work? How do we know that Philus is clever?

Sentences 5 How do we know that Volubilis is a very good cook?

Sentences 6 How do we know that Bregans is not as clever as Philus? What does he want to do?

Sentences 7 **a** What does Loquax have?

b Complete this translation: Loquax _____ sweetly.

Sentences 8 **a** How is Anti-Loquax described?

b Complete this translation: Anti-Loquax _____ _____ very well.

Sentences 9 **a** How are the slaves described (two words)?

b Complete this translation: The slaves _____ to work.

Check

trēs servī p. 5

Work out the meaning in your head and then read the play aloud.

Exercise Who made the following statements? What do they mean? Complete the following table.

Statement	Person	Translation
ego ad Ītaliam redīre volō.		
fessus sum.		
ego aquam bibere nōn possum!		
ego labōrāre nōlō.		
nōs sōlem numquam vidēmus!		
semper pluit!		
ego dormīre volō.		
nūllum vīnum videō.		
ego sōlem vidēre volō.		
nōs dē hāc coniūrātiōne audīre volumus.		

Check

Note on the new words in the margin

You may have noticed that some of the new words are presented in a slightly different way. New nouns are given in the form in which they appear in the story, e.g. **sōlem**, followed by the nominative singular and meaning, **sōl** *sun*. If new nouns occur in the story in the nominative singular, this is the only form that is given.

New verbs are also given in their form in the story, e.g. **lavat**, followed by a new part of the verb, **lavāre** (which will be explained on p. 10), and the basic meaning of the verb, *wash*. You will have to work out that **lavat** means *he washes*.

The slaves p. 20

Large numbers of Britons were enslaved at the time of the Roman conquest and after the revolt of Boudica. Those that worked in the mines and on farm estates were often very badly treated and sometimes kept in chains (see the pictures on p. 5).

The Britons, too, kept and exported slaves before the Romans came and used the same type of slave chains.

Read **The slaves**, p. 20, to find out more.

Salvius p. 21

Read this section. You will find that some details are known about Salvius' life, but very little has come down to us about his character or what he did in Britain. The stories about him in Book II keep to the known facts but are largely invented.

coniūrātiō p. 7

In this story Salvius inspects an iron mine in Kent.

Read lines 1–10 then answer the following questions.

1 Why was Salvius in the territory of the Cantici?

2 His host was Pompeius Optatus. What sort of person was he?

3 **Salvius nōn erat contentus** (line 5). Why was it strange that Salvius was not satisfied?

4 Why did Salvius pick on one of the slaves?

5 What did he say about **servōs inūtilēs** (line 8)?

6 What did he do about the slave he picked on?

Write out a translation of lines 11–21.

Read lines 22 to the end and then answer the questions.

7 Pompeius Optatus was shocked by Salvius' behaviour. What does he say in line 24?

8 What accusation does Salvius make about the guards?

9 Do you think he was right? (Look back at lines 17–18, if necessary.)

10 What did Pompeius do? Which word in the last sentence tells you that he really disagreed with Salvius?

Check

Pictures p. 6   Study the pictures and text which show how the site of an iron mine in Kent has been identified. One of the main reasons that attracted the Romans to Britain was its wealth of mineral resources (see the map on p. 40).

About the language 1: infinitives pp. 10–11

Para. 1   Read.

Para. 2   Translate the examples in your head and write down the infinitive in each example.

Para. 3   Learn the present tenses of **volō** and **nōlō**. Why is **nōlō** easy to learn?

Now learn **possum**. The last part of each of the forms of **possum** should be familiar to you. Why? For help turn to p. 162 and look at the present tense of **sum** and **possum**.

Para. 4   Read.

Para. 5   Test your knowledge by translating the examples without looking up any words.

Check

Bregāns pp. 8–9

Look at the cartoon version of the story on p. 5 of this book. If you have time you should read the whole story and answer the questions on p. 9.

Salvius fundum inspicit p. 12

Read lines 1–21 then answer the following questions.

1 What did Varica show Salvius first on their tour of the farm?

2 **seges est optima** (line 3). What proof did Varica give of this?

3 The picture shows what Salvius expected to see. Why was he disappointed (lines 5–9)?

4 How did Varica try to defend Cervix (lines 12–13)?

5 What effect did this have on Salvius? What did he want to do with Cervix?

6 Why were the two slaves going to the barn (lines 15–18)?

7 Why was Salvius displeased when he heard the answer?

Write out a translation of lines 22 to the end.

General question 8 You have now met Salvius and Varica several times. How would you describe them and why? Try to think of several aspects of each character, both good and bad. If you are in a group you could divide the characters between you and then compare your descriptions.

Check

About the language 2: -que p. 13

Paras. 1 and 2 Read and then rewrite examples **a** and **b** in paragraph 1, using **-que** instead of **et**.

Para. 3 Translate the further examples. Then rewrite these examples in Latin using **et** instead of **-que**.

Check

Practising the language pp. 14–15

Ex. 1 Write out this exercise. You should use each infinitive in the box only once. Check your answers. If you have made more than two mistakes in the second sentence of each pair, read the language note on p. 10 again.

Ex. 2 Write out the exercise as instructed.

Ex. 3 Revise the verb forms in the box and their meanings before attempting this exercise. If you need help, see p. 160. Then write out the exercise.

Check

Farms in Roman Britain pp. 16–17

Re-read this section. Then consider the following situation.

You were born twenty years after the Romans came to Britain and your father is a prosperous British farmer. You suggest that he replaces the family roundhouse with a farmhouse in the Roman style (see the drawing below). Your father is violently opposed to the idea and threatens to disinherit you. His arguments boil down to the following:

1 Why should we change from the ways of our ancestors to imitate these upstart and arrogant Romans?

2 We know how to build and repair our British houses. We can supply all the materials from our land. I'd rather spend our wealth improving our farm or buying high-status objects to impress our neighbours. (See the gold torc on p. 22.)

3 Our house is easy to keep warm. We have a big hearth and oven and our entrance faces south-east and gets all the morning sun.

4 How would we smoke our meat and keep down the vermin in the thatch if we didn't have a fire in the house?

5 How could I see what was going on if we lived in one of these newfangled houses with separate rooms?

You decide to wait until your father calms down before you approach him again. What do you say then to try to win him over?

Check

The economy of the farm pp. 18–19

Study this section and the accompanying pictures and revise **Farms in Roman Britain**, pp. 16–17. Then answer the following questions.

1 Why might a family have chosen to settle in this spot?

2 What crops are grown, or likely to be grown, on this farm?

3 What animals were used to pull the plough? Extra clue: look at p. 19.

4 What animal products can this farm supply? Think of things to wear and use as well as to eat.

5 What everyday things would the farm not provide?

6 How would the farmer have obtained these?

7 What other buildings might there have been near the farmhouse? What would they have been used for?

 Check

Revision

Present, imperfect and perfect tenses p. 160

Revise the first three tenses in the table.

1 Test yourself by writing out in full from memory:

    a the present tense **trahō**

    b the imperfect tense **audiēbam**

    c the perfect tense **docuī**.

2 Without looking at the table translate the following examples:

    a portābam; portāvit; docēmus; docuistis.

    b audīs; trahēbant; portātis; audīvī.

    c docēbat; portāvistī; trāximus; audiunt.

3 Translate the following examples:

    a ambulābat; ambulāvērunt; manēmus; manēbātis.

    b dūxī; dūcit; pūnīvērunt; pūniēbam.

    c sedeō; laudāvistis; venīs; mittēbant.

 Check

Vocabulary p. 171

Read paragraph 6 before learning the checklist on p. 22. This explains that the verbs in the following vocabulary and in the checklists are given in a different way from those in Book I.

Work through the examples in paragraphs 7 and 8. If you have problems refer again to the table of verbs on p. 160.

 Check

Vocabulary checklist 13 p. 22

Learn the checklist, including all parts of the verbs. Then answer these questions. Use an English dictionary to help you if necessary.

1 What is an *edifice*?

2 What is *alternative* medicine?

3 What Latin word do *incantation* (English) and *chanter* (French) come from? Clue: What can Loquax do?

4 *Etc.* is a common abbreviation. What is the whole phrase? What does it mean?

5 If a burglar receives a *custodial* sentence, what happens to him?

6 Why is the *diction* of an air traffic controller important?

7 What is a *novel* solution to a problem?

8 If a contract is declared *null and void*, what does that mean?

9 Think of an English word beginning with *vita-*. What is its connection with **vīta**?

10 If you belong to a *voluntary* organisation what is special about it? Why is it called this?

11 What do we mean when we say that young children or old people are *vulnerable*?

12 Give the meaning of the following parts of the verbs you have learnt:

   advenīre; excitāvī; interficere; ruō.

Check

Language test

1 Rewrite the following sentences, using **-que** instead of **et**. Translate the sentences.

   a Salvius et Rūfilla in vīllā magnificā habitābant.

   b lībertus dominum et uxōrem excitāvit.

   c canis ex ōrdine ruit et Salvium petīvit.

   d custōdēs cubiculum intrāvērunt et Alātōrem interfēcērunt.

   e Salvius ad fundum advēnit quod agrōs et servōs īnspicere volēbat.

2 Complete the sentences by selecting a suitable infinitive from the box and then translate the sentences. There are many different possibilities.

currere	ambulāre	cantāre
pugnāre	recumbere	rīdēre
lacrimāre	manēre	

a _____ vult.

b _____ potestis.

c _____ nōlunt.

d _____ vīs.

e _____ possumus.

3 Read the following sentences. Translate the words and phrases in **bold type** and say what tense the verbs are. The first one is done for you.

Latin word or phrase	Translation	Tense
a **servī** ad horreum **festīnābant**.	The slaves were hurrying.	imperfect
b **Salvius** servum aegrum ē turbā **trāxit**.		
c dīligenter **labōrāvistis**, geminī.		
d in Britanniā sōlem numquam **vidēmus**.		
e **vīlicus** dominō agrōs **ostendēbat**.		
f cūr arātōribus cibum **dātis**?		
g dē hāc coniūrātiōne audīre **volumus**.		
h ubi sunt ancillae? nūllās ancillās **videō**.		
i cūr **saeviēbās**, domine?		
j **custōdēs** Alātōrem **interfēcērunt**.		

Check

Progress record   Textbook pp. 1–22   Student Study Book pp. 1–10

Stage 13 in Britanniā	Done	Revised	Any problems?
Model sentences			
trēs servī			
The slaves			
Salvius			
coniūrātiō			
About the language 1: infinitives			
Bregāns			
Salvius fundum īnspicit			
About the language 2: -que			
Practising the language			
Farms in Roman Britain			
The economy of the farm			
Revision			
Vocabulary note and Vocabulary checklist 13			
Language test			

Stage 14 apud Salvium

You have seen Salvius at work, visiting a new mine and inspecting his own estate. In this Stage he is with his wife Rufilla and their domestic slaves in their country villa.

Picture p. 23

This is a reconstruction of the kind of room Salvius and Rufilla may have had in their country villa. Most of the furniture, pottery and glass would have been imported. The walls are decorated in a style that was fashionable in Italy and were probably the work of an Italian painter.

Model sentences p. 24

Work out the meaning and answer the questions below.

amphoram: amphora	*wine-jar*
gravis	*heavy*

1 Who is giving orders? What authority does this person have?

2 Both Philus and Loquax give two reasons each for being unwilling to carry out the orders. What are these reasons?

3 The order given to Bregans is different from the orders to the other slaves. Which Latin words show this difference? The pictures will help you.

Read the Latin sentences aloud, dividing up the speakers if you are in a group.

Check

Roman amphorae

Roman amphorae were usually plain earthenware jars with two handles, one on each side of a long neck. They were often tall, with a solid 'toe' at the bottom so that they could be jammed upright in the ground or in a wooden rack.

The Romans used amphorae to store and transport wine, olive oil, honey, a fish sauce called **garum**, fruits like grapes and olives, and grain.

When the amphorae were filled, they were corked or stopped with plugs made of plaster, clay or wood. Those intended for export often had the abbreviation of the exporter's name stamped into their handles. Most of the amphorae found in Britain came from exporters in Gaul, Spain and Italy. Amphorae were sometimes reused as containers for the ashes of the dead, or, laid end to end (with holes broken in), as makeshift drainage pipes.

Rūfilla p. 25

Read lines 1–10 (**dīcēbās**) and then answer the questions.

1 Why do you think Rufilla sends the hairdressers out of the bedroom?

2 Why does Rufilla think Salvius is a cruel man (lines 4–7)?

3 Which Latin word in line 9 suggests that Rufilla is a nagging wife?

Read lines 10–15 (**ēlēgistī**)

4 Now compare the statements made by Rufilla and Salvius below with those you have just read. If the statements AGREE put A in the boxes; if they DISAGREE put D.

ego vīllam rūsticam habēre nōlēbam.

mox ego tibi vīllam dedī.

haec vīlla nōn prope urbem est.

ego ipse vīllam ēlēgī.

Work out the rest of the story, lines 15 to the end, in your head.

General question 5 In the table below are some English words describing the characters of Rufilla and Salvius as they appear in this story. Find ONE reason to support each description.

Character	Description	Reason
	changeable	
	complaining	
	spoilt	
	rich	
	generous	
	patient	

Check

Domitilla cubiculum parat I pp. 26–7

Translate this cartoon version of the story. If you have time read the full story. Translations are given in the *Answer Key*.

1
Domitilla, ubi es?

in hortō sum, Marcia. quid vīs? fessa sum, quod diū labōrāvī.

necesse est nōbīs cubiculum parāre. domina familiārem ad villam invītāvit. domina ipsa mē ad tē mīsit. necesse est tibi cubiculum verrere. necesse est mihi pavīmentum lavāre. quaere scōpās!

Marcia (anus)

2 Domitilla ad culīnam lentē ambulābat. īrāta erat, quod cubiculum verrere nōlēbat.

ego ōrnātrix sum. nōn decōrum est ōrnātrīcibus cubiculum verrere.

3
subitō Domitilla cōnsilium cēpit et ad culīnam quam celerrimē festīnāvit.

4 simulac culīnam intrāvit, lacrimīs sē trādidit.

5
mea columba, cūr lacrimās?

lacrimō quod miserrima sum. pertōtum diem labōrāvī. quam fessa sum! nunc necesse est mihi cubiculum parāre.

mea columba, nōlī lacrimāre! ego tibi cubiculum parāre possum.

Volūbilis, quam benignus es!

6 coquus cum ancillā ad cubiculum revēnit. dīligenter labōrāvit et cubiculum fēcit pūrum.

7
meum mel! meae dēliciae!

coquō ō sculum dedit.

8 coquus ērubēscēns ad culīnam revēnit.

14 *Stage 14*

Domitilla cubiculum parat II p. 27

Read lines 1–10 and then complete the sentences by filling in the gaps below.

1 Lines 1–2. Then Marcia entered the bedroom.

   The old woman _____

2 Line 6. Although she was astonished, Marcia _____

3 From lines 4–7 pick out a suitable sentence as a title for this picture and translate it.

Title: _____

Translation: _____

4 Domitilla told two lies because

   a (line 4) _____

   b (lines 9–10) _____

Read lines 11 to the end and then answer the questions.

5 Rufilla praises her slaves. What does she say (line 12)?

   _____

6 Why is Rufilla still not happy about the bedroom?

   _____

7 What solution does Domitilla suggest?

   _____

8 Which sentence tells you that Rufilla will go along with Domitilla's idea?

   _____

Check

Pictures pp. 26–7

Notice the basket-work chair on p. 26 and compare the drawings of furniture on p. 27 with the reconstructions on p. 23.

About the language 1: adjectives pp. 28–9

Paras. 1 and 2	Read.
Para. 3	Work out the meaning of the sentences in your head.
	Write down the Latin noun and adjective pairs and state their cases, as instructed.
Further practice	Complete the Latin sentence with the correct word and translate.

1 servus _____ amīcum vituperāvit. (īrātus, īrātō)

2 custōs puerum _____ laudāvit. (callidus, callidum)

3 dominus canī _____ cibum dedit. (fidēlis, fidēlī)

Check

Paras. 4 and 6	Read.
Para. 5	If you had no mistakes in paragraph 3 and in **Further practice**, work out in your head the sentences in this paragraph. Then, as instructed, write down the noun and adjective pairs and state whether they are singular or plural. If you did have mistakes, then write out this paragraph.
Para. 7	Translate these further examples.

Check

The Romans in Britain pp. 36–9

1 Read **The British tribes** and **The conquest**. In the table below are the names of people who were connected with the Roman conquest. Explain briefly what each one did and how successful they were.

Names	What did they do?	How successful were they?
Julius Caesar		
Claudius		
Aulus Plautius		
Agricola		

2 **The inscription, p. 37**

This is reprinted with a translation in the box below. Some of the inscription has been lost, but it is possible to reconstruct the meaning of the whole because many inscriptions are written in a set way. The English words which translate the Latin are printed in capitals.

TI · CLAV	To the Emperor TIBERIUS CLAUDIUS,
AVG	son of Drusus, Caesar AUGUSTUS Germanicus,
PONTIFIC	High PRIEST,
COS · V · IM	CONSUL for the FIFTH time, saluted as IMPERATOR twelve times:
SENATVS · PO	the SENATE and PEOPLE of Rome set this up because
REGES · BRIT	he received the surrender of eleven BRITISH KINGS
VLLA · IACTV	who were defeated without ANY LOSS
GENTESQVE	AND because he brought barbarian PEOPLES
PRIMVS · INDIC	FIRST under Roman RULE.

Claudius had five names: Tiberius Claudius Caesar Augustus Germanicus. Imperator usually means Emperor, but it was also the title given to a Roman commander after a great victory.

3 Read **Romanisation and trade**, pp. 37–8, and **Imports and exports**, p. 40, using the map to clarify the roads, areas and products mentioned. Now answer these questions.

  a Give TWO reasons why the building of roads was important to the Romans.

  b Suggest TWO reasons why the Britons might have welcomed the Romans and TWO reasons why they might have opposed them.

4 Look at the pictures in Stages 13 and 14 and make a note of any imported and exported goods and any you think may have been produced in Britain for the British market.

5 Read **Boudica**, pp. 38–9, and answer these questions.

  a Why was Boudica nearly successful?

  b Why were the Romans fascinated by her?

  c What archaeological evidence is there for her campaign?

  d Why do you think the sculpture (p. 38) was made?

Check

in tablīnō p. 30

In this story you will discover the identity of Rufilla's visitor. Can you guess who it is? Clue: He appeared in Book I.

Read lines 1–15 before answering the following questions.

1 In what way is Salvius **occupātus**?

2 Why do you think Rufilla addresses him as **mī Salvī** and **mī cārissime**?

3 What mood is Salvius in? Why?

4 Why is Salvius not able to find his chair and cupboard? What else do you know is missing from the study?

Read lines 16–28 and write out a translation.

5 Here is a translation of lines 29 to the end. Read it together with the Latin.

> *Salvius:* *What did you say? You invited a Pompeian? To our house?*
> *Rufilla:* *It's right for me to invite my relation here. The slave-girls have prepared a bedroom for my relation. Because the bedroom was unattractive, the slave-girls put your chair and cupboard in it.*
> *Salvius:* *You are crazy, wife! The Pompeians are bigger liars than the Britons. You didn't take the chair and cupboard from the study, did you?*
> *Rufilla:* *And the lamp-stand.*
> *Salvius:* *Heavens above! Oh my lamp-stand! Oh dear!*

Use your translation of lines 16–28 and the translation above to answer the following questions.

6 Why is Rufilla pleased about the forthcoming visit?

7 Why does Salvius not like the idea?

Check

About the language 2: more about adjectives p. 31

Paras. 1 and 2   These give you more information about adjectives. Read carefully how the adjectives of different declensions work.

Para. 3   Translate the examples as instructed. Then write the Latin noun and adjective pairs in the box below and state their case and number.

	Noun	Adjective	Case	Singular or plural
a				
b				
c				
d				
e				
f				

Further examples

Work out the meaning of the following sentences and pick out the noun and adjective pairs. Write them in the box below.

1 dominus fābulam longam nārrābat.

2 custōdēs ferōcēs in cubiculum ruērunt.

3 puerī multās bēstiās vīdērunt.

4 mercātor amīcō fessō vīnum dedit.

5 cēterī lībertī in viā ambulābant.

Noun	Adjective
1	
2	
3	
4	
5	

What differences can you see in the pairs of adjectives and nouns in the two boxes? Why are they different?

 Check

Quīntus advenit p. 32

1 Work out the meaning of lines 1–16 and then translate these sentences:

a exspectātissimus es! (line 3)

b cēnam modicam tibi parāvī. (line 7)

c post cēnam cubiculum tibi ostendere volō. (lines 8–9)

d nōnne illa clādēs terribilis erat? (line 13)

e cūr Quīntum nostrum vexās? (line 15)

2 Work out the meaning of lines 17 to the end. In the following translation some mistakes have been made deliberately. Underline the English words or phrases which are wrong and write them out correctly. There are SIX mistakes altogether.

Rufilla spoke to Quintus.

'Perhaps my dear Quintus is tired. We have prepared a bedroom for you. The bedroom is not elaborately furnished. In it are a little cupboard and a small lamp-stand.'

Salvius now spoke angrily.

After he saw the bedroom, Quintus cried out,

'The bedroom is also tasteful! I have seen nothing more tasteful.'

'You are lucky', said Salvius. 'Your bedroom is more tasteful than my study.'

3 Answer the questions at the bottom of p. 32. If you are in a group, you could divide the first question between you.

4 In the box is a list of adjectives that could be used to describe Salvius or Rufilla in this story.

| charming | hospitable | self-controlled | tactless | considerate |

Choose TWO that you think suitable for Salvius and TWO for Rufilla and give the evidence for your choice.

		Adjective	Evidence
Salvius	a		
	b		
Rufilla	a		
	b		

Check

Practising the language p. 35

Ex. 1 Write out as instructed.

Ex. 2 Write out as instructed. If you are unsure of the meaning of the forms, look at p. 162 before doing this exercise.

Check

Britain in the first century AD p. 40

1 From the stories that you have read, you know that Salvius and Rufilla and their household are well established in Britain. Look at the map and then answer these questions about places which have been mentioned in Stages 13 and 14. Write down the Latin name for

a the city that Rufilla missed so much

b the town near which Salvius' villa may have been sited

c the tribal area where Salvius had the slaves executed.

2 Find out the English names for the places marked on the map and write them in the spaces provided. One place-name, Wroxeter, has been done for you. The first letter of the other names has been given to you. Use an atlas to help you if necessary.

Check

tripodes argenteī pp. 33–4

1 Work out the meaning of lines 1–14. Then complete these sentences by filling in the missing words.

    a _____ has to go to the palace.

    b _____ visiting _____ today?

    c Every year _____ because _____

    _____ .

    d _____ the emperor who _____

    _____ .

    e _____ the situation.

    f Those _____ .

2 Read lines 15 to the end, in which we are told how Salvius and his steward try to find a suitable present for Cogidubnus. The possible presents are shown below. Write down why each one at first seems suitable and then unsuitable.

    a    **b**    **c**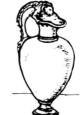

3 What present does Salvius finally decide to take? What is Quintus taking to the king? Why is his present a better one than Salvius'?

Check

Roman tripods

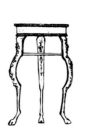 

Tripods ranged from the very simple to the ornate and expensive like the ones in the picture. They were fitted with a tray or bowl at the top. They were often used in religious ceremonies to make offerings of food and wine to the gods or to burn incense.

Some tripods had folding legs so that they could be easily transported.

Important events and dates p. 41

Study the chart and then answer the following questions. You may need to refer to pp. 36–9 as well.

1 Why are the three Romans portrayed here important in the history of Britain?

2 What message is the coin meant to give?

3 To which events do the bottom two pictures refer?

Check

Vocabulary checklist 14 p. 42

Learn the checklist. Then answer the questions.

1 When a mistake is *deleted*, what is done to it?

2 The Romans, after the death of an emperor, would *deify* him. How would they then regard him?

3 When you *donate* something, what are you doing?

4 What sort of a person is a friend who shows great *fidelity*? What is *hi-fi* short for and what does it mean?

5 Salvius and Rufilla do not live together in *marital* harmony. What does this mean?

6 Why would you expect Cogidubnus to have a *regal* appearance?

7 Match the Latin words with their meanings by placing the correct letters in the spaces. The first one is done for you.

a	iste		among
b	-que		how
c	ubi		himself
d	quamquam		and
e	ipse		when
f	aliquid		although
g	quam		something
h	apud	a	that

Check

Language test

1 Fill in the correct word and translate the sentences.

a marītus stolam _____ uxōrī ēmit. (pulchram, pulchrās)

b amphorās _____ ad vīllam portābant. (ingentem, ingentēs)

c dominus _____ servum cotīdiē verberābat. (crūdēlis, crūdēlēs)

d rēx amīcō _____ dōnum dedit. (fidēlis, fidēlī)

e centuriō _____ custōdēs spectābat. (attonitus, attonitō)

2 Translate these sentences.

a decōrum est mihi rēgem vīsitāre.

b quam magnifica est aula!

c num servum ignāvum retinēre vīs?

d quamquam domina ipsa nōs spectat, dīligenter labōrāre nōn possumus.

e servī ancillaeque, ubi dominum vīdērunt, eum salūtāvērunt.

3 Match up each Latin verb form in the column on the left by putting its letter next to the correct English translation on the right. The first one is done for you.

a	interfēcistī		I say
b	ruēbant		they arrived
c	dēlēvimus		they are able
d	advenīre		you want
e	possunt	**a**	you killed
f	dīcō		I said
g	vultis		to arrive
h	interficit		we destroyed
i	dīxī		they were rushing
j	advēnērunt		he kills

Revision

Nouns

	first declension	second declension	third declension	
SINGULAR				
nominative	puella	servus	mercātor	leō
accusative	puellam	servum	mercātōrem	leōnem
dative	puellae	servō	mercātōrī	leōnī
PLURAL				
nominative	puellae	servī	mercātōrēs	leōnēs
accusative	puellās	servōs	mercātōrēs	leōnēs
dative	puellīs	servīs	mercātōribus	leōnibus

First revise the key nouns above. Then do the following exercises:

1 Change the words in **bold type** from the singular to the plural and translate the new sentence.

For example: **servus** in fundō **labōrābat.**

This becomes: **servī** in fundō **labōrābant.**

Translation: *The slaves were working on the farm.*

a **mercātor** ad urbem **contendēbat.**

b **ancilla** dominam in ātriō **exspectābat.**

c **centuriō** fūrem ferōciter **pulsābat.**

d **coquus** cēnam splendidam **parābat.**

2 Change the words in **bold type** from the plural to the singular and translate again.

    a servī epistulās longās **scrībēbant**.

    b leōnēs aquam **bibēbant**.

    c pictōrēs mūrōs **pingēbant**.

    d fīliae mātrem **vocābant**.

3 Translate the following sentences; then write down the case and number (singular or plural) of the nouns shown in **bold type**. See if you can do this exercise without looking at the table of nouns.

	Translation	Case	Number
a Rūfilla **marītum** saepe vexāvit.			
b Quīntus dōnum **rēgī** comparāvit.			
c **custōdēs** in cubiculum ruērunt.			
d domina stolās **ancillīs** ēmit.			
e taurus **servōs** terruit.			
f ubi **mercātōrem** vīdistī?			
g puerī **leōnibus** cibum dedērunt.			
h lībertus amīcīs **canēs** ostendit.			

Check

Progress record   Textbook pp. 23–42   Student Study Book pp. 12–25

Stage 14 apud Salvium	Done	Revised	Any problems?
Model sentences			
Roman amphorae			
Rūfilla			
Domitilla cubiculum parat I			
Domitilla cubiculum parat II			
About the language 1: adjectives			
The Romans in Britain			
in tablīnō			
About the language 2: more about adjectives			
Quīntus advenit			
Practising the language			
Britain in the first century AD			
tripodes argenteī			
Important events and dates			
Vocabulary checklist 14			
Language test			
Revision			

Stage 15 rēx Cogidubnus

In this Stage you will meet Cogidubnus, the British king, who has invited important Romans and Britons to a ceremony at his palace. He had helped the Romans to conquer southern England and had been given Roman citizenship. How can you tell this from the picture?

 Check

Picture p. 43

This is a photograph of an important inscription that was found at Chichester. You will learn more about it in the background section. In the meantime can you pick out the letters that give us part of Cogidubnus' name?

Check

Model sentences pp. 44–5

Study sentences 1–3 and look at the pictures. You can probably guess the new words. See if you can answer these questions:

Sentences 1 What was Cogidubnus holding?

Sentences 2 How would you recognise the queen?

Sentences 3 What did Cogidubnus feel about one of the presents he was given?

Now see if you can fill in the gaps in this translation of the model sentences.

Sentences 1 The old man, _____, was King Cogidubnus.

Sentences 2 A woman was sitting near Cogidubnus. The woman, _____ _____, was the queen.

Sentences 3 Many Romans were giving expensive things to Cogidubnus. The present, _____, was a horse.

Study sentences 4–6.

paterā: patera	*bowl*
vīnum lībāvit	*made an offering of wine*
āram: āra	*altar*
bālāvit: bālāre	*bleat*

Now fill in the gaps in the translation of some of the sentences.

Sentences 4 The wine, _____, was in
a golden bowl.

Sentences 5 The lamb, _____, was the
victim.

Sentences 6 The victim, _____,
bleated.

Check

ad aulam pp. 46–7

1 Read lines 1–6 which describe the procession to King Cogidubnus' palace.
Then match the objects below with the people who carried them in the
procession. Which picture and group of people are the odd ones out? Give
a reason for your choice of picture and people.

A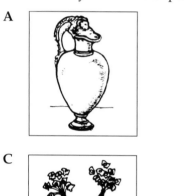

B

C

D

2 Read lines 7–31 and answer these questions.

a **magna turba erat in viā** (lines 7–8). Who were in the crowd?

b What did Varica tell Salvius? What question did he ask him?

c **nōn decōrum ... exspectat** (lines 14–16). Find TWO reasons in these lines
why Salvius was angry with the Britons.

d How did Varica carry out his orders (lines 17–19)?

e What did many of the Britons do? What did the two young men do (lines
20–2)?

f Look at the picture. From lines
26–31 pick out the group of FOUR
words that describes it.

g For whom were the young men
waiting? Why?

3 Work out the meaning of lines 32 to the end. In these lines the characters are described in the following ways. Can you explain why?

Line	Character and description	Reason
32	Vārica anxius	
36	Salvius … īrātior quam anteā	
43	iuvenēs … attonitī	
46	Salvius … cachinnāns	
46	Britannī … molestissimī	

Check

caerimōnia pp. 48–9

Look at the picture on pp. 46–7.

When Salvius and Quintus arrived at the palace they would first go into the pillared entrance hall and then be conducted across the garden to a grand atrium, where the king would receive them and his many other visitors. The story describes a very strange ceremony that took place in the palace.

Read lines 1–15 and answer questions 1–5. If you are in a group you may like to work in pairs.

Read lines 16 to the end and answer questions 6–12.

Picture question

Label the picture above with these words: **rēx**, **puer**, **rogus**, **effigiēs**, **spectātōrēs**, **fax**. If you were asked to add the **aquila** what would it be?

Check

Cogidubnus, king of the Regnenses pp. 55–6

Read this section and then write down an entry for Cogidubnus in 'Who's Who in Roman Britain'. You may like to add to this when you have read Stage 16.

Full name:
Address:
Titles:
Tribe:
Citizenship:
Religion:
Career:
Interests:

Check

About the language 1: relative clauses p. 50

Paras. 1 and 2   Read.

> In the second example in paragraph 2 **quod** means *which*. You have previously met **quod** meaning *because*. The sense of the sentence will tell you which is the correct meaning. For example, the translation 'Near the young men was a wagon, because it was blocking the whole road' would not make sense.

Para. 3   Translate the examples and complete the exercise as instructed.

Check

lūdī fūnebrēs I p. 51

After the ceremony commemorating Claudius' funeral, the day ended with an athletic competition and boat-race in his honour. Holding 'funeral games' was a Greek and Roman custom. Cogidubnus perhaps wanted to show Salvius and the other Romans his admiration of Roman ways as well as his respect for the Emperor Claudius.

1   Read this translation of lines 1–7.

> *After the ceremony King Cogidubnus led a procession to the shore. There the Britons celebrated the funeral games. There were present the Regnenses, the Cantici and other British tribes.*
>
> *The competitors competed with one another for a long time. The Cantici were very happy, because they were always victorious. A Cantican athlete, who ran very fast, easily beat the rest. Another Cantican athlete, who was very skilful, threw the discus further than the others.*

2   Read lines 8–11 and then complete the table below with details in English about the competitors and their captains.

The competitors	Captain	His character
Cantici		
Regnenses		

Read lines 12–15.

3   What were the sailors waiting for?

4   Write down TWO Latin words which indicate how quickly the boats set off.

5   What did the spectators do?

Check

lūdī fūnebrēs II p. 52

Read lines 1–9 and then answer the questions.

1 Translate the captions on the map.

2 The course of one of the captains is marked on the map. Which one?

3 Mark in the course of the other captain up to this point in the story (line 9).

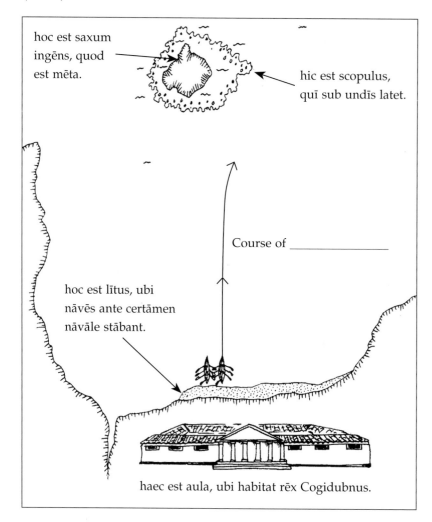

hoc est saxum ingēns, quod est mēta.

hic est scopulus, quī sub undīs latet.

Course of _____

hoc est lītus, ubi nāvēs ante certāmen nāvāle stābant.

haec est aula, ubi habitat rēx Cogidubnus.

Read lines 10–20 (**pervēnit**) and then answer the questions.

4 What did Belimicus say about himself and his crew and about the Regnenses (lines 10–12)?

5 Who reached the turning point first?

6 **subitō nāvis Cantica in scopulum incurrit** (lines 15–16). Why did this happen?

7 What TWO other things happened to the **nāvis Cantica** (lines 16–18)?

8 What happened to Dumnorix and his ship (lines 19–20)?

9 On the map chart the rest of the course taken by each ship from its position in line 9.

Write out a translation of lines 20 (**multī**) to the end.

Check

About the language 2: imperfect tense of *possum*, etc. p. 53

Paras. 1 and 2   Read.

Para. 3   Learn the imperfect forms of **possum**.

> Note that the last part of each of the forms of **poteram** is the same as the imperfect tense of **sum**: **eram**, **erās**, etc.

Para. 4   Work out the meaning of the sentences in your head.

Paras. 5 and 6   Read the examples and write out translations.
Check

Practising the language p. 54

Ex. 1   Write out sentences **a–c** and check your answers. If you have got them right, finish the exercise in your head. If not, revise the forms of the nouns on p. 24 of this book and then write out the rest of the exercise.

Ex. 2   Work out in your head sentences **a**, **c**, **e** and **g**. Write out sentences **b**, **d**, **f** and **h**.

Further work   1   How can you recognise an *infinitive*?

2   Pick out the Latin infinitives from the sentences in exercise 2.
Check

Vespasian and the Durotriges p. 57

Study the pictures and the captions. The archaeologists found thirty-seven skeletons buried with food for their journey to the next world. The picture on p. 58 shows an arrowhead that has stuck in the spine of a defender.

You can see the area where the Durotriges lived and where Maiden Castle and Hod Hill are on the map on p. 40.

Vocabulary checklist 15 p. 58

Learn the checklist and answer the following questions:

1   Give an example of an *aquatic* sport.

2   If someone has been *excluded* from an activity, would he feel pleased or not?

3   What sort of person is a *debtor*?

4   *Canine* is to **canis** as *equine* is to _____. What do the English words mean?

5   What is an *impediment*?

6   A *marina* is

    a   a lady from Mars;

    b   a place for mooring boats;

    c   an exotic cocktail?

7 Who uses *nautical* miles?

8 Why is the head of a college sometimes called a *principal*?

9 What do the following verb forms mean: **redeō, redīre, rediī**?

10 How would you describe a *tenacious* person? Why are some occupants of houses called *tenants*?

11 What should *undulating* country remind you of?

12 Julius Caesar said 'I came, I saw, I conquered'. You have now met these three words in Latin. What are they?

Check

Language test

1 Complete each sentence by using a group of words from the box below. Then translate the sentences.

> quī rēx Britannicus erat
> quae antīquissima erat
> quod tōtam viam complēbat
> quod in mediīs undīs erat
> quem servus tenēbat
> quae in lītore stābat

a tandem Salvius urnam, _____, ēlēgit.

b sacerdōs agnum, _____, sacrificāvit.

c agmen, _____, ad aulam prōcēdēbat.

d Cogidubnus, _____, prīncipēs ad caerimōniam invītāvit.

e magna turba, _____, lūdōs fūnebrēs spectābat.

f nāvēs saxum, _____, petīvērunt.

2 Translate the following imaginary report sent to Cogidubnus by Vespasian after he defeated the Durotriges. New words are given below.

> grātiās maximās tibi agō quod mihi auxilium dedistī. mīlitibus frūmentum comparāvistī; ad mē explōrātōrēs mīsistī. hī explōrātōrēs nōs ad regiōnem dūxērunt, ubi Durotrigēs habitābant.
>
> Durotrigēs fortiter pugnāvērunt, sed nōs eōs mox superāvimus. multōs Durotrigēs necāvimus; multās fēminās līberōsque cēpimus; multōs vīcōs incendimus. nōs fortiōrēs erāmus quam barbarī. facile erat nōbīs eōs superāre.

explōrātōrēs: explōrātor	*scout, spy*
regiōnem: regiō	*region*
vīcōs: vīcus	*village*
incendimus: incendere	*burn, set fire to*

Check

Revision

Irregular verbs pp. 162–3

First study the present and imperfect tenses of **ferō** *I bring*, which you have not seen set out in a table before, and learn them.

Then learn the present and imperfect tenses of **sum**, **possum** and **volō**.

- The present tense of **possum** is made up of **pos-** or **pot-** meaning *able* and the present tense of **sum** *I am*. Similarly, **poteram** *I was able* is made up of **pot-** and **eram** *I was*.

- The tenses of **nōlō**, *I do not want*, work in the same way as **volō**, *I want*, except for a few differences in the present tense (see p. 10).

1 What are the present tense forms of these words: **poterat**; **poterātis**; **poterant**?

2 What is the Latin for: we are able; you (singular) are able; I was able?

3 What are the present tense forms of these words: **nōlēbam**; **volēbant**; **nōlēbāmus**?

4 What is the Latin for: you (pl.) did not want; I wanted; you (s.) want; he does not want?

5 Choose the right word from the box to complete each of the Latin sentences. Then translate the sentences. Be careful to translate the tenses correctly.

poterāmus	volēbam	fert
nōlunt	ferēbātis	nōn vīs

a ego dormīre ....

b servī labōrāre ....

c nōs vincere ....

d puer cibum ....

e tū audīre ....

f ancillae, cūr flōrēs .... ?

 Check

Progress record
Textbook pp. 43–58   Student Study Book pp. 27–35

Stage 15 rēx Cogidubnus	Done	Revised	Any problems?
Model sentences			
ad aulam			
caerimōnia			
Cogidubnus, king of the Regnenses			
About the language 1: relative clauses			
lūdī fūnebrēs I			
lūdī fūnebrēs II			
About the language 2: imperfect tense of **possum**, etc.			
Practising the language			
Vespasian and the Durotriges			
Vocabulary checklist 15			
Language test			
Revision			

Stage 16 in aulā

In Stage 15 you met the client king, Cogidubnus, and saw his close relationship with the Romans. In this Stage you will discover the magnificence of the palace, possibly given to him by the Emperor Vespasian. The pictures on pp. 59–63 and 69–74 illustrate the splendour of the building, its decorations and the garden, and show the extravagant banquets and entertainments held there. The drawing on the right shows the impressive entrance hall of the palace.

Picture p. 59

This shows the entrance to the great audience chamber in the palace where Cogidubnus would receive Salvius and Quintus and other guests. You can see how the whole palace was laid out on p. 69.

Model sentences pp. 60–1

Read sentences 1–3 and work out the meaning.
Sentences 1 and 2 each contain a new verb form. Can you spot it and give the meaning?

importāverat: importāre	*import*
fōns	*fountain*
marmoreus	*made of marble*
effundēbat: effundere	*pour out*

Work out the meaning of sentences 4–6.

ōvum	*egg*
posuērunt: pōnere	*put, place*
appāruit: appārēre	*appear*
saltātrīx	*dancing-girl*
pūmiliōnēs: pūmiliō	*dwarf*
pilās: pila	*ball*
iactābant: iactāre	*throw, toss*

Exercise   When you have done this, fill in the gaps in these sentences.

Sentences 4   The dinner, _____ _____
_____, was very good.

Sentence 5   From the egg, _____ _____
_____, appeared a dancing-girl.

Sentences 6   Then the dwarfs, _____ _____
_____, came in.

Each of the Latin relative clauses you have translated above contains the new form of the verb. Write down the Latin verbs and check the meaning you have given in your translation.

Check

Belimicus ultor p. 62

Read lines 1–14 and then answer the questions.

1   What would be a good translation for **rem** (line 2)?

2   Why was Belimicus' own tribe, the Cantici, jeering at him?

3   How did the slaves react? Why do you think they did this **clam** (line 5)?

4   Who is Belimicus speaking to in lines 6–8? Is what he says a true account of what happened? Give a reason for your answer.

5   **multae bēstiae** (line 10). How had they come to the palace?

6   What job did the German slave have?

Read lines 15 to the end.

7   How did Belimicus tame the bear?

8   What entertainment was announced by Cogidubnus?

9   What further steps did Belimicus take in his plan to get his own back on Dumnorix? What do you think he is going to do (lines 19–25)?

10   Who is described as **invītus** (line 24)? Suggest a reason for this.

Check

About the language: pluperfect tense p. 66

Paras. 1 and 2   Read and examine carefully the pluperfect tense. You will observe that it has the same first part or *stem* as the perfect tense: e.g. perfect tense: **portāvit**; pluperfect tense: **portāverat**.

The endings for the pluperfect tense are quite easy to remember. Try saying them aloud without looking at your book.

> Note the meaning of the pluperfect tense: e.g. **importāverat**: he *had* imported. Compare this with the meaning of the perfect tense: **importāvit**: he imported or he *has* imported.

Further examples 1 Translate into English: **excitāverat; vēnerant; dūxerāmus; tenuerās**.

2 Translate these perfect tenses and then change them into the pluperfect and translate again: **clāmāvit; īnspexērunt; trādidistis**.

Para. 3 Translate.

Para. 4 Read, observing especially the different way of forming the present tense as compared with the perfect and pluperfect tenses.

Para. 5 Work out the examples in your head.

Further exercise In the box below are four verbs in different tenses. Match each of the verbs to the most suitable word in the table, to describe the time of the action and to make good sense. Translate the completed sentences.

| effūgērunt | spectābās |
| advēnerat | labōrō |

Completed sentences	Translation
hodiē	
diū	
subitō	
ōlim	

Check

rēx spectāculum dat I p. 63

1 Read lines 1–3. Which Latin sentence would be a suitable caption for this picture?

Read lines 4 to the end and find evidence from the story to support the truth of these statements. Answer in English.

2 Dumnorix enjoyed 'getting at' Belimicus.

3 Belimicus did not lose his temper.

4 Not all the guests were pleased with the king's show.

5 The dwarfs and dancing-girls were not the only entertainment that was expected.

Check

rēx spectāculum dat II pp. 64–5

Work out the meaning of lines 1–15 and answer questions 1–4.
Finish reading the story and answer questions 5–12.

Further work   These English translations are incorrect. Decide what the mistakes are and write down the correct version.

Lines	Incorrect translation	Corrected version
7–8	I am jeering at you, because you dare not handle the bear.	
11–12	Surely you cannot show the guests the bear?	
14–15	You also, little man, can overpower it.	

Finally, you could tape-record the story. Remember to put in suitable sound effects.

Check

The palace at Fishbourne pp. 68–73

Before reading the information, study the model and the captions on p. 69. This will give you a good idea of the size and layout of the building and garden, as well as its elaborate design and nearness to the sea.

Now read the whole section and study the pictures. Then answer these questions.

1   What would you have been able to see on the site of Fishbourne in the following years: AD 44; AD 70; AD 79?

2   Archaeologists have found remains of materials on the site. When the palace was being built, what parts of it would the following have been used for:

   a   marble

   b   coloured stone

   c   iron?

3   What evidence is there to suggest that the owner wanted his palace and gardens to imitate those in Italy?

4 **a** Where would you expect to find the following? Label the picture with the appropriate letter.

    A   a hypocaust

    B   visitors entering the palace

    C   amphorae being unloaded

    D   the owner receiving important officials

    E   underground pipes

    F   guest rooms

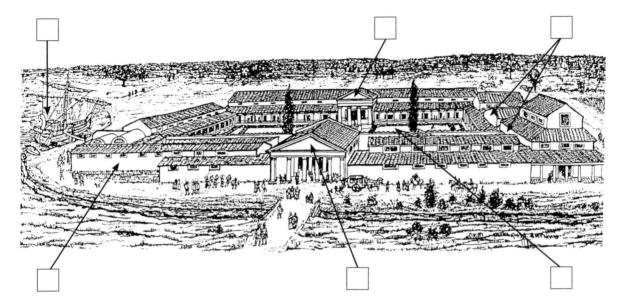

b Which part of the building, which you have labelled above, was there before the palace was built?

Check

Quīntus dē sē p. 67

Quintus has saved the king's life and he and Cogidubnus have become good friends. Cogidubnus is interested in Quintus' experiences at the time of the destruction of Pompeii and afterwards.

Read lines 1–13 and answer the following questions. You need not write out the answers. If you are in a group you could work them out together.

1 Where did the king have this conversation with Quintus?

2 Who escaped with Quintus (lines 6–8)?

3 How did Quintus raise money after the eruption of Vesuvius?

4 Why did he want to leave Italy?

Now read the rest of the story.

5 a On the map write in the square boxes the numbers 1, 2, 3, 4, to indicate
      the order of the places Quintus went to after escaping from Pompeii.

   b Now mark in the rectangular boxes the *Latin* names of the countries.
      All except one are in the story. Remember to use the nominative of the
      word.

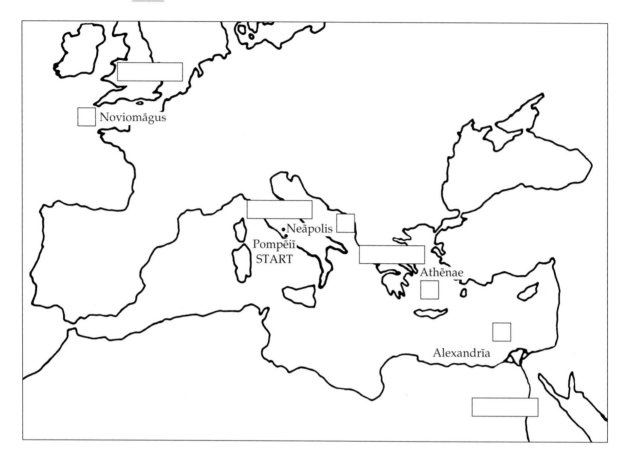

Practising the language p. 68

Do the exercise as instructed. If you are uncertain about the pluperfect endings,
turn to p. 66 and revise them before you start.

Check

Vocabulary checklist 16 p. 74

1 What is an *auxiliary* nurse?

2 Why would you feel pleased to receive a *bonus*?

3 Sometimes in a meeting there is a *consensus* of opinion. What does this
   mean?

4 If you are given a *delectable bonbon*, what would you do with it? Why?

5 What is a *floral* arrangement?

6 What would you be doing if you were trying to *ameliorate* a situation?

7 What is *navigable* water?

8 Some plastics are practically *imperishable*. What does this mean?

9 What would someone be doing if he was *imposing* a task on you? If you were asked in a shop for a *deposit*, what would you have to do?

10 There were many *converts* to Christianity in the Roman Empire. What does this mean?

 Check

Language test

1 Below is a list of various forms from four different verbs in the checklist. Write the forms in the correct columns below. One verb has been started for you.

  a cōnsentiēbāmus, cōnsentīre, cōnsēnsistis

  b nāvigābāmus, nāvigō, nāvigāre, nāvigāveram, nāvigāvērunt

  c posuerās, pōnere, pōnunt

  d tollis, sustulit, sustulerātis, tollēbant, tollere

Present tense	Imperfect tense	Perfect tense	Pluperfect tense	Infinitive
a	cōnsentiēbāmus			
b				
c				
d				

Now write out the meanings of the verb forms in **d** above.

2 Translate the sentences:

  a necesse erat imperātōrī fabrōs ignāvōs, quōs pūnīverat, dīmittere.

  b num in aulā saltāre vultis?

  c postrīdiē ego, quod ad vīllam redīre nōlēbam, ad lītus effūgī.

  d nōnne decōrum erat nōbīs Cogidubnum laudāre, quī nōbīs cēnam splendidam dederat?

  e quamquam rēx tibi nōn favet, eum honōrāre dēbēs.

 Check

Revision

Pronouns I pp. 156–7

Paras. 1 and 2   Revise the pronouns, noticing the similarities between the forms of **ego** and **tū** and **nōs** and **vōs**.

Paras. 3 to 5   Read and write out a translation of the further examples in paragraph 4.

Para. 6   Read. Now work out the following examples in your head and then write down the meaning of **sē** or **sibi** in each sentence.

    a   Belimicus ex aquā **sē** trāxit.

    b   fēmina cibum **sibi** comparāvit.

    c   Rōmānī semper **sē** laudābant.

    d   coquus cēnam splendidam **sibi** parābat.

Longer sentences I pp. 167–8

Paras. 1 and 2   Revise sentences with **postquam**.

Para. 3   Write out a translation of the *Further examples*. See if you can translate them into the more natural English form given in paragraphs 1 and 2.

Para. 4   Revise sentences with **quamquam** and **simulac**.

Para. 5   Work out in your head the meanings of the first short sentence in each example, but write out the longer sentences in full.

Progress record

Stage 16 in aulā	Done	Revised	Any problems?
Model sentences			
Belimicus ultor			
About the language: pluperfect tense			
rēx spectāculum dat I			
rēx spectāculum dat II			
The palace at Fishbourne			
Quīntus dē sē			
Practising the language			
Vocabulary checklist 16			
Language test			
Revision			

Stage 17 Alexandrīa

In Stage 17 the scene moves to Egypt, a part of the Roman Empire that is very different from Roman Britain. Although the people have now generally accepted Roman rule, there are still many problems and much unrest. The stories are set in Alexandria, a large, wealthy and prosperous city, in which can be found many different races with conflicting needs and attitudes.

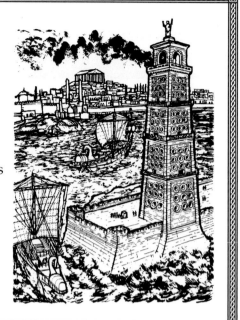

The events are described by Quintus in the form of a flashback which covers the years from AD 79 (the eruption of Vesuvius) to AD 82 when he arrived in Britain.

Picture p. 75

An Alexandrian coin showing the Pharos, the lighthouse at Alexandria, which was one of the seven wonders of the ancient world. This coin provides some of the evidence for the appearance of the Pharos. See the drawing above and the pictures on p. 88.

Model sentences pp. 76–7

Quintus is telling Cogidubnus what happened after he arrived in Alexandria with Clemens, who is now a freedman.

Work out the meaning of the sentences and answer the questions.

Sentences 1 a What TWO things are we told about the position of the lighthouse?

b Where are there a lot of ships?

Sentences 2 a Name THREE sets of people who can be found in the **ingēns turba**.

b Why are the soldiers in Alexandria?

Sentences 3 a How did the temple come to be in Alexandria?

b Who hurried to this temple?

c Where was the altar?

d Who poured the wine?

Sentences 4 a How did Quintus know Barbillus?

b **patre meō**. What was this person's name?

Sentences 5 a **Barbillus … nūllōs**. Why did Quintus need to obtain a slave?

b Translate the sentence which shows that the slave was not newly bought for Quintus.

Check

dē vītā Quīntī

Fill in the gaps in these sentences about the life of Quintus. Use the story **Quīntus dē sē** on p. 67 and the model sentences on pp. 76–7 to help you.

1 Quintus inherited estates in _____. ☐

2 Quintus was welcomed by a rich merchant in _____. ☐

3 He described his travels to a king in _____. ☐

4 He heard many philosophers arguing with one another in _____. ☐

When you have done this, put the events in chronological order by putting 1, 2, 3, 4 in the boxes.

Check

tumultus I p. 78

1 Translate lines 1–4, remembering that it is Quintus who is telling the story.

2 Read lines 5–10 (**multitūdō**) and then write down in English what the following people were doing:

People	Activity (in English)
a mercātōrēs	
b fēminae et ancillae	
c tabernāriī	
d multī servī	

3 Read this translation of lines 10–11.

At last we arrived at the harbour of Alexandria. Very many Egyptians were there, but we could not see any Greeks.

From this point there is a growing feeling of fear and suspense. Work out the meaning of the rest of the story in your head and note down the Latin words or phrases that create this feeling.

Although both Quintus and the slave-boy feel the menace, they have different ideas about what to do. What do they each want to do and why?

Check

tumultus II pp. 78–9

Read lines 1–13 and answer questions 1–4.
Read lines 14–21 and answer questions 5–8.
Read lines 22 to the end and answer questions 9 and 10.

Further work Look again at lines 5–10 and write down:

a one perfect tense   **b** one imperfect tense

c one pluperfect tense   **d** one infinitive

e one relative clause

Check

About the language: genitive case p. 80

Para. 1 Read this paragraph which tells you about a new noun form, the genitive case. The genitive is often translated by the English word 'of' and generally expresses possession or 'belonging to', e.g. the house of Barbillus.

Para. 2 Study the forms of the genitive and learn them. Now turn to p. 150.

> Notice that **puellae**, the genitive singular, is the same as the dative singular and nominative plural; and **servī**, the genitive singular, is the same as the nominative plural.

When you are reading a sentence, the sense and the word order will usually make clear which form a word is in. You will see this in the following sentences. Translate them and then give the cases of the words in **bold type**.

1 multī **lībertī** in urbe labōrābant.

2 Quīntus ad tabernam **lībertī** contendit.

3 in casā **puellae** erat canis ingēns.

4 iuvenis ānulum **puellae** dedit.

Para. 3 Translate.

Further exercises 1 In each sentence in the table below, underline the English words which would be in the Latin genitive. Then write down the correct Latin genitive form and state what other Latin form or forms, if any, would look the same. If you need help, consult pp. 150–1.

English sentences	Latin genitive	Other forms
Quintus saw the body of the boy.		
The dresses of the women were very beautiful.		
The windows of the house had been broken.		
We examined the goods of the merchant.		

2 Look back at **tumultus II**, pp. 78–9. In lines 1–15 there are FOUR DIFFERENT nouns in the genitive case. Read these lines carefully and write down the genitives with their meanings.

> • Be careful not to confuse the genitive plural forms with the accusative singular forms which you already know, e.g.:
>
> | | second declension | third declension |
> |---|---|---|
> | *Acc. sing.* | servum | leōnem |
> | *Gen. pl.* | servōrum | leōnum |
>
> • It is often more natural in English to express the genitive by 's or s' rather than by *of*, e.g. the girl's book (= the book of the girl), the slaves' tunics (= the tunics of the slaves).

Check

Alexandria pp. 86–91

In the model sentences and in **tumultus** you are given a picture of Alexandria as a great city and port, seething with racial tension. Read pages 86–7, as far as the end of the first paragraph, and study the map on p. 87, which shows Alexandria's importance as a meeting-place of several trade routes.

Now see if you can chart the voyage of a merchant living in Athens who has the following contracts:

A cargo of copper for a wholesaler in Alexandria.

A consignment of oil for a workshop in Africa.

A delivery of silks and perfumes to a shopkeeper in Hispania (Spain).

Four horses for a rich man in Massilia.

Pottery for a wholesaler in Ostia.

Bales of linen for a factory in Alexandria.

A cargo of ivory for a shop in Athens.

The merchant fulfils his contracts in the order given above. Mark his journey on the map.

In the small boxes number in order the places where he loads or unloads his goods.

In the large boxes write the goods he would load (**L**) and unload (**UL**) at each place, e.g. **OIL – L, OIL – UL**. The first one is done for you.

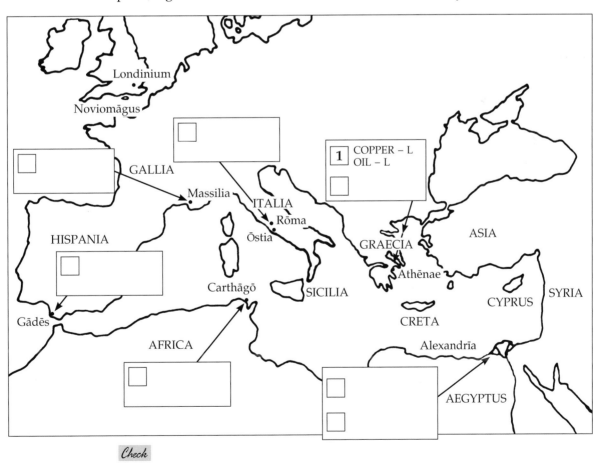

Check

ad templum pp. 81–2

The temple in the story is that of the Egyptian god Serapis, who was the god of the harvest and agriculture. The picture on p. 82 shows a head of Serapis, found in a temple in London. Notice the symbol on the god's head.

Read lines 1–4 and answer the questions.

1 **per ... ībam**. Translate this sentence. Who is telling the story and to whom?

2 How does the description in lines 1–2 reflect what you have already read about Alexandria?

3 Look at the pictures on p. 81 and read the caption. What nationalities might you add to the list in line 2?

Read lines 5–14 and answer the questions.

4 Why does Barbillus say **ēheu**?

5 Why is Barbillus described as **invītus** (line 10)?

6 **ad templum Augustī** (line 11). Where have you heard of this temple before in this Stage?

7 Translate the reply of Barbillus (lines 12–14).

Read the translation of lines 15–20 along with the Latin.

> Plancus: *I am on holiday today. It is all right (convenient) for me to go to the temple of Serapis. I can tell you about Serapis.*
> *(Plancus started going along with us, chattering. He began to tell us about all the monuments.)*
>
> Barbillus: (whispering) *Our friend is more talkative than a parrot and more obstinate than an ass.*

8 Look again at the Latin text, lines 15–20. Write down

  a TWO Latin words in the dative case;

  b TWO infinitives;

  c TWO comparative adjectives.

Read lines 21 to the end and answer the questions.

9 What question does Plancus ask (line 23)?

10 **canistrum** (line 24). What would such a basket or measure normally contain?

11 **opportūnē hūc vēnimus** (lines 25–6). Why does Plancus say this?

12 Lines 30–1. Who are being addressed? Which of the pictures on p. 82 would make a suitable illustration for the speaker?

13 **rīdēns** (line 33). How have Barbillus' feelings changed from the way he was described in lines 5 and 10? What has caused this change?

14 If you were acting this scene, how would you make Plancus sound particularly irritating?

Check

Ancient worship

In the story the priests came out of the temple to tell the crowd to be silent as a sacrifice was about to take place. The sacrificial animal would then be killed at the altar in front of the temple. This was the usual procedure. People did not attend services inside temples as Christians do in churches or Moslems in mosques. The purpose of a temple was to be a home for a particular god and to house his statue and any offerings made to him. Worship generally took place outside in the open air.

Alexandria continued

Turn to p. 87 and read the paragraph beginning 'Travellers from Greece or Italy' about the Pharos and look again at the pictures and captions on p. 88. Recent underwater explorations, which are still continuing, have revealed masonry and statues from the Great Harbour at Alexandria, including a huge figure which may have stood by the Pharos (see the pictures on p. 91).

Read the rest of the background material. You will be able to find most of the places described on the panorama of Alexandria on pp. 84–5.

Picture p. 90 This is the kind of mosaic Barbillus might have had in his richly decorated villa. The design of the Gorgon's head would face the doorway of the dining-room. The parts of the floor that would be covered by the dining-couches have a plainer design. This is one of the ways that helps to identify a dining-room in a Roman house.

Now answer the following questions.

1 In the table are four types of people who would have been excited by what Alexandria had to offer. Write down ONE physical feature of the city which would have interested each type and explain why. If you are in a group, you could divide the work between you and then compare answers.

Person	Interesting feature	Reason
a merchant		
a tourist		
a scholar		
an architect		

2 What differences would Quintus have found between life in Alexandria and his previous life in Pompeii?

 Check

Practising the language p. 83

Ex. 1 This exercise gives more practice with the genitive case. Write out as instructed.

Ex. 2 Write out the answers as instructed for sentences **a–d**.

Check

If you made no mistakes in these, work out the answers for sentences **e–h** in your head. Otherwise, write these out also.

Ex. 3 First write down the Latin words at the top of the exercise and their English meanings. Write out the sentences as instructed.

Check

Vocabulary checklist 17 p. 92

Read the information at the top of the page. Note especially that nouns will now be listed with the nominative singular first, as in previous checklists, and also with the *genitive singular* which you have just learned in Stage 17, e.g. **animus**, nominative singular; **animī**, genitive singular (meaning *of the spirit*).

Write down and learn all the noun forms in the checklist. (The form of **negōtium** will be explained later.) Now answer the questions.

1   Which Latin word gives the English *fabric* and French *fabrique* (meaning *factory* or *workshop*)? What is the connection?

2   Why are the British sometimes described as *insular*?

3   After long *negotiations* the workers were awarded a pay rise. What are *negotiations*?

Learn the rest of the words including all the parts of the verbs and answer these questions.

4   What do these verbs mean: **absum**; **abeō**? You have not yet met the verb **abdūcō**, but can you work out what it means?

5   How is the meaning of **appropinquō** connected with that of **prope**?

6   What is a *benefactor*? If you had a *benign* grandmother, what sort of person would she be?

7   If you have the right equipment for a job, it will *facilitate* the work. What does this mean?

8   The defendant was acquitted because of the *paucity* of the evidence. Explain why he was not convicted.

9   What do these verb forms mean: **pervenīre**; **recēpī**; **resistō**?

10 You have learnt the words in the table below in previous checklists. Now that you have met the genitive case, can you write down the genitive singular and plural?

Nominative	Genitive singular	Genitive plural
aqua		
marītus		
unda		
imperātor		
deus		

Check

Language test

1 Tick the correct Latin form of the words in **bold type** in the English sentences.

   a The slave-girl was arranging the hair **of her mistress**. (dominae, dominārum)

   b We heard the shouts **of the boys**. (puerī, puerōrum)

   c They discovered the **centurion's** plan. (centuriōnis, centuriōnum)

   d The boy had broken the soldier's **spear**. (hastam, hastae)

   e The young man stole the lady's **jewels**. (gemmās, gemmārum)

   f They boldly entered the **lions'** den. (leōnem, leōnum)

2 Translate the sentences:

   a nostrī amīcī, quī diū nāvigāverant, tandem ad portum pervēnērunt.

   b stolās sordidās emere numquam dēbēmus.

   c nōnne fabrī āram prope templum aedificāverant?

   d itaque ancillae, quās domina hūc mīserat, hospitēs dēlectāvērunt.

   e Britannī igitur flōrēs statuāsque in hortō rēgis spectābant.

   f multī Graecī fūgērunt; paucī restitērunt.

   g Barbillus quondam negōtium cum patre Quīntī agēbat.

3 Study the Latin nouns in the pool below. Then complete the table on the left.

You will have to put some Latin nouns alongside more than one case.

Case	Latin nouns	Pool of Latin nouns	
accusative singular		rēgem	pecūniam
genitive singular		mercātōris	lībertō
dative singular		nautās	gladiātōrī
nominative plural		spectātōrēs	equī
accusative plural		custōdum	dominae
genitive plural		cibum	puerōrum

Check

Revision

Verbs pp. 160–1

Revise carefully the four tenses of the four conjugations.

Paras. 1–3 Do the examples as instructed.

Further examples Pick out the 'odd one' and give your reason.

1 aedificāvit, audit, dūxit, mīsit

2 trādis, sentis, respondēs, venītis

3 spectat, videt, laudāverat, vulnerat.

Persons and endings

Para. 1 This is a useful summary of all the verb endings. Read the information and learn the table.

Para. 2 Do the examples as instructed.

Further examples Below are the descriptions of three Latin words. What are the words and what do they mean?

1 3rd person plural perfect of **audiō**.

Latin word: _____

Translation: _____

2 1st person singular imperfect of **trahō**.

Latin word: _____

Translation: _____

3 2nd person plural pluperfect of **portō**.

Latin word: _____

Translation: _____

Irregular verbs pp. 162–3

p. 162 You have previously revised the present and imperfect tenses of the four verbs. Check that you remember the forms.

Now study the perfect and pluperfect tenses and the infinitives and learn them. You will meet the perfect and pluperfect tenses of **sum** later.

p. 163 Read paragraphs 1 and 2; then, without looking at the tables opposite, translate the examples in paragraph 3.

Further exercises **1** With your book closed, complete the words by putting in the missing letter from the list. Translate the words.

List of letters: a i ō u l m s t

Latin word	Translation
e( )tis	_____
vu( )t	_____
erā( )us	_____
potuēr( )nt	_____
( )ulistī	_____
fer( )mus	_____
vol( )	_____
pot( )it	_____

2 Solve these jumbled words, then translate your answers:

terf, sumsop, solivuti, level, brasea.

Check

Progress record

Stage 17 Alexandrīa	Done	Revised	Any problems?
Model sentences			
dē vītā Quīntī			
tumultus I			
tumultus II			
About the language: genitive case			
Alexandria			
ad templum			
Ancient worship			
Alexandria continued			
Practising the language			
Vocabulary checklist 17			
Language test			
Revision			

Stage 18 Eutychus et Clēmēns

In this Stage Clemens becomes a shopkeeper in Alexandria. He soon finds himself a victim of the local mafia, headed by a thug called Eutychus, but refuses to give in to them. The picture shows Clemens on the right confronting Eutychus and two of his henchmen.

Picture p. 93

The fragments of shattered glass symbolise the violence of Eutychus and his thugs which is described in this Stage. When you read the stories you will see why the glass is particularly relevant.

taberna p. 95

Quintus spent a long time looking for a shop for Clemens. Read lines 1–6 and then answer the following questions about the shop he found.

1 Who did the shop belong to?

2 Where was it?

3 What would you expect this shop to sell?

4 What advantage did it have?

Look at the picture; then read lines 7–12 in which Barbillus tells Quintus about the dangers of owning a shop in this part of the city.

5 Why did the shopkeepers fear the **latrōnēs** (lines 7–8)?

6 Who is the old man in the picture?

7 Why was he attacked?

8 What happened to him and his shop?

Quintus is not put off by Barbillus' warning. Read lines 13 to the end of the story.

9 Why does Quintus think that Clemens can cope (lines 13–14)? Give TWO reasons.

10 Why do you think that Barbillus did not haggle about the price?

11 Translate the sentence that shows you that Quintus bought the shop.

12 Vocabulary check. In the story you met the following verbs from previous checklists. Can you remember them? **quaerō**; **interficiō**; **teneō**; **inveniō**; **necō**.

Check

Glassmaking in Alexandria pp. 105–7

Read this section and study the pictures.

1 Complete the paragraph below by choosing the right words from the box.

cooled	trailing	chemicals
brown	clay	semi-liquid
sand	core	sodium carbonate

Glass is made from _____ and _____.
When heated it becomes _____ but hardens again
when _____. Perfume containers and small vessels used to be
made by moulding. A _____ was made of _____ and
sand, already formed into the shape of the vessel; molten glass was poured
round this and left to cool. The glass could be made different colours by
adding _____ to make blue, green, _____ and white.
Decoration was often added by _____ lines of molten glass onto
the finished article.

2 a Look at the picture. Describe what the workmen marked **A**, **B** and **C** are doing.

A _____

B _____

C _____

b Label the following tools:

    i two pairs of SHEARS for cutting the molten glass;

    ii TONGS;

    iii DIVIDERS for measuring the glass;

    iv a MOULD into which glass would be blown.

3 Look at these two vases. Can you describe how they would be made?

    a   **b**

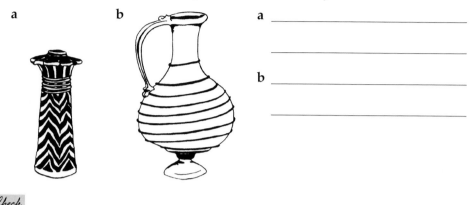

a _____

b _____

Check

in officīnā Eutychī I p. 96

Read this translation of lines 1–3.

> *After I gave the shop to Clemens, he thanked me very warmly. He immediately hurried to the street in which the shop was: so much did he want to own a shop.*

Read lines 4 to the end. Then answer the following questions about the characters.

1 **īrātus ... Clēmēns** (line 6). Why was Clemens angry?

2 **tabernārius ... perterritus** (line 9). Why was the shopkeeper frightened?

3 **servī Aegyptiī** (line 12). Most people would have been afraid of them. Why?

4 **eōs tamen nōn timēbat** (lines 13–14). How did Clemens show that he was not afraid of the slaves (lines 14–end)?

5 Why does Clemens call the slave Atlas? Look at the picture on p. 122.

6 **servōs attonitōs** (line 18). Why were the slaves astonished?

Check

Alexandria, home of luxury glass p. 97

The blue and white disc forms the base of a famous glass vase, the Portland vase, which you can see in the British Museum. The person portrayed on the disc is Paris. He is looking thoughtful because he has to decide which of the goddesses Juno, Minerva or Venus is the most beautiful.

in officīnā Eutychī II pp. 96–7

We now meet Eutychus. Read lines 1–11 and then answer these questions about him.

1 What picture do you get of Eutychus in lines 1–2?

2 Is he polite or rude to Clemens (line 4)? Give a reason for your answer.

3 Why do you think Eutychus changed his attitude after Clemens explained why he had come (lines 5–9)?

4 Eutychus took Clemens on a tour of his workshop. Why is it unlikely that the workshop shown on p. 106 belonged to Eutychus (lines 9–11)?

Eutychus now decides to negotiate with Clemens. Write out a translation of lines 12–19.

Read lines 20 to the end. Clemens is not taken in by Eutychus.

5 Which Latin word in lines 21–2 tells you that Clemens turned down Eutychus' offer?

6 What reason did Clemens give?

7 sēcūrus (line 22). Is this what you might expect Clemens to feel? Give a reason for your answer.

Check

Clēmēns tabernārius pp. 98–9

Read the story and answer the questions on p. 99.

Further exercises 1 Look at lines 8–12 again. Pick out SEVEN Latin words or phrases that are connected with the worship of the goddess.

2 There are FOUR infinitives in the story. Find them and give their meaning. If you need to revise infinitives see p. 160.

Check

About the language: gender pp. 100–1

Paras. 1–3 Read.

Para. 4 Write out the exercise as instructed.

Para. 5 Read.

Further exercise Translate the following sentences:

a Clēmēns, quī pius erat, ad templum Īsidis cotīdiē adībat.

b sacerdōtēs, quī templum administrābant, Clēmentem mox cognōvērunt.

c fēlēs, quae sacra erat, in cellā templī habitābat.

d templum, quod Clēmēns saepe vīsitābat, prope tabernam erat.

In each sentence pick out the Latin word for 'who' or 'which' and the word it describes. What gender is each pair?

Para. 6 Read.

Further exercises 1 Now write down the meaning and gender of the following nouns in the table below. You will have to look up the gender of nouns that are not obviously masculine or feminine.

Noun	Meaning	Gender
domina		
fīlius		
mōns		
īnsula		
agmen		
gladius		
āra		
pars		
flōs		
mare		
lībertus		

2 Look at the nouns and their genders. What do you notice about the gender of nouns ending in **-a** and **-us**?

Check

Egypt pp. 108–9

1 Read this section.

2 At the end of the section you will have found a list of the bribes paid by a Greek living in Egypt.

gift	240 drachmas
to the guard	20 drachmas
bribes	2,200 drachmas
to two police agents	100 drachmas
to Hermias, police agent	100 drachmas
to a soldier	500 drachmas

Suggest FOUR reasons why bribes might be offered. The description of life in Egypt and the stories in this Stage will help you. If you are in a group, you could pool ideas.

3 The man who actually made the list did not write down the reasons for the bribes and gave the name of only one of the people to whom he paid them. How do you account for this?

Check

prō tabernā Clēmentis p. 102

Translate this cartoon version of the story in your head. You will need to use the vocabulary on p. 102.

quondam Clēmēns, ubi ā templō, in quō cēnāverēat, domum redībat, amīcum cōnspexit accurrentem.

taberna ardet! taberna tua ardet! tabernam tuam dīripiunt Eutychus et latrōnēs. eōs vidī valvās ēvellentēs, vitrum frangentēs, tabernam incendentēs. fuge! fuge ex urbe! Eutychus tē interficere vult. nēmō eī latrōnibusque resistere potest.

Clēmēns tamen nōn fūgit, sed ad tabernam quam celerrimē contendit. valvās ēvulsās, tabernam dīreptam vīdit. Eutychus extrā tabernam cum latrōnibus Aegyptiīs stābat, rīdēbatque.

VITRUM

mī dulcissime! nōnne tē dē hāc viā monuī? nōnne amīcōs habēs quōs vocāre potes? cūr absunt? fortasse sapientiōrēs sunt quam tū.

absunt amīcī, sed deī mē servāre possunt. deī hominēs scelestōs pūnīre solent.

quid dīcis? tūne mihi ita dīcere audēs?

tum Eutychus latrōnibus signum dedit. statim quattuor Aegyptiī cum fūstibus Clēmentī appropinquābant. Clēmēns cōnstitit. via, in quā stābat, erat dēserta. tabernāriī perterritī per valvās tabernārum spectābant. omnēs invītī Clēmentem dēseruerant, simulatque Eutychus et latrōnēs advēnērunt.

WHAT HAPPENED TO CLEMENS?

Read the rest of the story on p. 102, lines 27–37, and either write out a translation or draw another cartoon.

Check

Egyptian cats p. 103

Study the pictures and read the text.

Practising the language p. 104

Ex. 1   First read the instructions at the top of the exercise. Then write out the sentences.

Ex. 2   Write out examples **a–c** and translate as instructed, and then check your answers. If all three are correct, do the rest in your head.

Ex. 3   Write out this exercise as instructed.

The verbs in brackets are all in the pluperfect tense.

Check

Vocabulary checklist 18 p. 110

Learn the checklist and do the following exercises.

1   Words of opposite meaning. By placing the correct letters in the middle column, match the checklist words with their opposites in the right-hand column. The first one is done for you.

Checklist word	Letter	Opposite word
a posteā		perveniō
b audeō		deus
c recūsō		timeō
d dea		pēs
e discēdō	a	anteā
f manus		volō

2   Words of a similar meaning. By placing the correct letters in the middle column, match the checklist words to those of similar meaning in the right-hand column.

Checklist word	Letter	Similar word
a obstō		rogō
b nam		nōlō
c petō		ostendō
d dēmōnstrō		enim
e discēdō		impediō
f recūsō		abeō

3 Several English words are derived from **manus**. Match the derivations with the clues given on the right. Put the letters in the boxes.

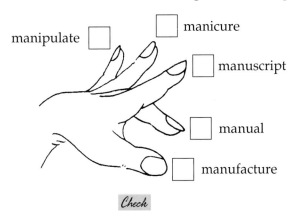

manipulate ☐

manicure ☐

manuscript ☐

manual ☐

manufacture ☐

Check

A Keep this instruction book close to hand.

B Beautiful hands may be the result.

C Rufilla often seems to do this to Salvius.

D The abbreviation is MS.

E Nowadays, people don't always use their hands to do this.

Language test

1 Read the following sentences. Underline the noun and adjective pair in each sentence and complete the table by giving the case, number (singular or plural) and gender of each pair. The gender of three of the pairs has been done for you.

		Case	Number	Gender
a	senex fortis cum latrōnibus frūstrā pugnāvit.			
b	ingēns turba prope tabernam Clēmentis stābat.			f.
c	Eutychus officīnam maximam Clēmentī ostendit.			f.
d	in officīnā Eutychī lībertus multōs fabrōs vīdit.			
e	multī latrōnēs tabernāriōs semper terrēbant.			
f	Clēmēns ōrnāmentum vitreum deae saepe cōnsecrābat.			n.

2 Complete the following sentences with the correct adjective from the box

Adjectives must agree with their nouns in case, number and gender.

fortis	bonōs
fortēs	bonum

a Barbillus puerum _____ Quīntō dedit.

b Eutychus amīcōs _____ nōn habēbat.

c lībertus _____ auxilium tabernāriīs dedit.

d tabernāriī nōn erant _____.

Now complete sentences **e–h** in the same way.

sacram	ingentēs
sacrum	ingentem

e Clēmēns saepe fēlem (f.) _____ in templō vidēbat.

f latrōnēs fūstēs _____ tenēbant.

g Clēmēns servum _____ ex ōrdine trāxit.

h sacerdōtēs librum (m.) _____ lībertō dedērunt.

Now translate sentences **a–h**.

Check

Revision

Word order pp. 165–6

In this section you will see how varied the order of words is in Latin sentences. The sentences will also give you more practice with verb tenses.

Paras. 1–4   Read and translate the further examples in your head.

Paras. 5 and 6   Read and write out the further examples.

Which one of the four tenses did not appear in any of the examples in paragraphs 1–6?

General question   Why do you think that there can be many different sorts of word order in Latin but not in English?

Longer sentences I p. 168

At the end of Stage 16 you revised work on longer sentences in paragraphs 1–5. Now work through paragraphs 6 and 7 which give you more practice in different types of longer sentences.

Check

Progress record   Textbook pp. 93–110   Student Study Book pp. 57–65

Stage 18 Eutychus et Clēmēns	Done	Revised	Any problems?
taberna			
Glassmaking in Alexandria			
in officīnā Eutychī I			
Alexandria, home of luxury glass			
in officīnā Eutychī II			
Clēmēns tabernārius			
About the language: gender			
Egypt			
prō tabernā Clēmentis			
Egyptian cats			
Practising the language			
Vocabulary checklist 18			
Language test			
Revision			

Stage 19 Īsis

The ancient Egyptians worshipped many
deities. You have read that Quintus
visited the temple of Serapis and how
Clemens joined the followers of Isis. In
Stage 19 the stories describe the festival
of Isis which took place in early spring.
In the picture the statue of Isis is being
carried in procession. On her head is a
sacred disc, representing the sun, and in
her hands are other sacred symbols.

Picture p. 111

This drawing on papyrus which dates from about 1050 BC shows another way
of portraying Isis. She holds a sceptre in her right hand, and an ankh (symbol of
life) in her left. Above her head is a throne which is her name in hieroglyphs.

The worship of Isis pp. 126–7

To find out more about Isis and her festival, read these pages and study the
pictures and captions. Then answer the following questions.

1 What special power did the Egyptians believe Isis had? Why was this
   important to them?

2 Why was her festival held at the beginning of spring? Give TWO reasons.

3 Where was the statue taken after the procession through the streets?

4 You should now be able to recognise what Isis is wearing on her head in
   the pictures on pp. 126–7. What are they? Note that Isis also wears a vulture
   headdress in the picture on p. 127.

Check

Model sentences pp. 112–13

Read sentences 1–3 and answer the following questions in Latin. Here is an
example:

quis est amīcus Barbillī?

Aristō est amīcus Barbillī.

Sentences 1 ubi habitat Aristō?

Sentences 2 quis est Galatēa? quid saepe facit Galatēa?

Sentences 3 quis est Helena? cūr multī iuvenēs Helenam amant?

Read sentences 4–7. Answer these questions in English. You should be able to guess the new words.

Sentences 4 How do the Alexandrians feel about the procession?

Sentences 5 Which features of the procession most interest Aristo and
and 6 Helena?

Sentences 7 What are the two young men interested in?

Read p. 112 again and write down the meaning of these words in the Latin sentences.

miserrimus	
haec	
numquam	
pulcherrima	

Now read p. 113 again and write down the meanings of these words.

hī	
prō pompā	
hās	
gerunt	

Check

Aristō p. 114

Read the story and tick the correct word(s).

1 Aristo is miserable / very miserable.

2 His father is dead / alive.

3 Writing tragedies brought fame to Aristo / his father.

4 Aristo wants a life that is peaceful / riotous.

5 His house is noisy / quiet.

6 He is always escaping from his wife / her friends.

7 Helena has many boyfriends / girlfriends.

8 Her friends are ill-mannered / refined.

Check

diēs fēstus I p. 115

Read the story and answer these questions by putting T (True), F (False) or U (Unknown) in the boxes.

1 In line 2 **iam** refers to winter time. ☐

2 Most of the Alexandrians wanted to watch the procession. ☐

3 Aristo and Barbillus took Quintus to see the procession. ☐

4 Galatea told Helena to hurry. ☐

5 Galatea told Aristo to move out of her path. ☐

6 Galatea and her party were in great danger. ☐

Check

diēs fēstus II pp. 116–17

Read lines 1–13 and then answer questions 1–7 on p. 117.
Now read lines 14 to the end and answer the rest of the questions.

Further exercise Read the Latin sentences and translate them. Write down who spoke the words and to whom they were spoken.

Line	Sentences	Translation	Spoken by	Spoken to
10	nōnne servum ēmīsistī?			
17	nōlīte nōbīs obstāre!			
22	ecce pompa!			

Check

Pictures pp. 115–17

These mummy portraits and many others found in Egypt show young people. It may be that the portraits were painted some years before they died, but we know from census returns that many people died young.

pompa pp. 119–20

Translate this cartoon version of the story. You will need to use the vocabulary on pp. 119–20.

pompa adveniēbat. prō pompā currēbant multae puellae, quae flōrēs in viam spargēbant. post multitūdinem puellārum tubicinēs et puerī prōcēdēbant. puerī suāviter cantābant. tubicinēs tubās īnflābant. nōs, quī pompam plānē vidēre poterāmus, assiduē plaudēbāmus.

duo iuvenēs tamen, quōs Galatēa ē locō ēmōverat, pompam vidēre vix poterant.

subitō iuvenēs, quī effigiem vidēre nōn poterant, Galatēam trūsērunt. iuvenis forte pedem Galatēae calcāvit.

Further exercise In the table are some adjectives which could describe several of the characters in the story. For each adjective write down TWO characters and for each character support your choice with ONE piece of evidence. If you are in a group you could divide this exercise between you. At the end share your findings.

Adjective	Character	Evidence
tolerant	1	
	2	
complaining	1	
	2	
appreciative	1	
	2	
rude	1	
	2	

Check

About the language 1: *hic* and *ille* p. 118

Paras. 1–3 Read and study the examples. Write down the case and gender of the words in **bold type** and whether they are singular or plural.

Para. 1

Latin word	Case	Gender	Singular/plural
hic			
hanc			
hae			
hōs			

Para. 2

illa			
illōs			
illae			
illud			

Para. 4 Translate the sentences in your head without looking at paragraphs 1 and 2.

Further exercises 1 From the table in paragraph 1 choose the correct form of **hic, haec, hoc** to agree with the following nouns.

    a _____ fēmina

    b _____ iuvenem

    c _____ puerōs

    d _____ pater

2 From the table in paragraph 2 choose the correct form of **ille**, **illa**, **illud** to agree with the following nouns.

a _____ mīles

b _____ fīliās

c _____ fabrum

d _____ īnsulae

Check

The worship of Isis continued pp. 128–9

Read the rest of the information and answer the questions.

1 The picture on the right, which is a drawing of the wall-painting on p. 128, shows a sacrifice being made to Isis. The birds in the picture are ibises, which were considered sacred.

a What is the square object behind the birds?

b Where is it situated?

c How can you tell that the sacrifice is in honour of Isis?

d The statue of Isis is not shown in the picture. Where do you think it might be?

2

Contrast this Egyptian drawing of Isis with the Roman painting of her on p. 129. What differences do you see in

a the dress of the goddess

b the way she is posed

c the objects she is carrying?

3 The worship of Isis was known as a mystery religion. Why do you think it was described in this way?

4 There are parallels between the worship of Isis and Christianity. Suggest THREE features which you think are similar. Is the worship of Isis like any other religion that you know?

5

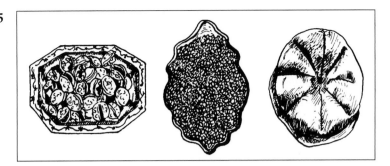

Archaeologists have found evidence to show that the worship of Isis was practised throughout the ancient world. Where was the food in the picture found? Why was it found there?

What else was found which added to the archaeologists' knowledge? (If you need help, read p. 129 again.)

6　The festival of Isis was a public holiday. What religious festivals today are celebrated in a similar way? What differences are there?

 Check

vēnātiō I p. 122

As well as worshipping deities such as Isis, the Egyptians also believed in astrology.

Read lines 1–15 and then answer these questions in your head.

1　What event had Barbillus arranged? Whom did he invite?

2　Who is Phormio? What is his part in the planned activity?

3　When did the astrologer run up? Why was he alarmed?

Write down the answers to the remaining questions.

4　Look at the drawing. Which THREE Latin words in the story could you use as a caption? What does the Latin mean?

5　Suggest a natural English translation for **mihi placet exīre** (line 12).

6　In the table below, write down the persons who did the actions and explain the reason for them.

Line	Action	Person	Reason
10	dērīsī		
11	cōgitāvit		
14	dedit		
15	contendimus		

7 Read this translation of lines 16 to the end.

When we arrived there, we saw many slaves gathered together. In this crowd of slaves were some Ethiopians, who were holding spears in their hands. Phormio, Barbillus' bailiff, was standing near the Ethiopians.

Phormio said, 'Hello, master! We have got everything ready for you. We have obtained the small boats which you asked for.'

'Did you kill the young goats?' asked Barbillus.

'We killed two young goats, master', answered the bailiff. 'We have already put them into the boats.'

Using the translation and the Latin text, write down an example of the following Latin forms:

a a word in the genitive

b a relative pronoun

c a word in the dative

d a noun and adjective pair

e a verb in the second person singular

f a verb in the second person plural

Check

vēnātiō II p. 123

1 Read lines 1–10 and fill in the words missing in the translation.

Then Phormio led us _____,
where the boats, _____, were tied up. After
_____, we sailed cautiously to the marsh,
in which the crocodiles _____.

When we _____ the middle of the swamp, Barbillus gave
a sign to Phormio. _____
into the water. When _____,
the crocodiles began to make headlong for them. Then the Ethiopians
_____ the crocodiles. They kept throwing their spears and kept
_____. The _____ of the crocodiles was
_____; however, _____ of the Ethiopians _____.
Soon many crocodiles _____.

2 Read lines 11 to the end of the story. To test your understanding, write down
from the pool of Latin words the correct answer for each action.

Pool	Latin word	Action
hippopotamus		woke up a hippopotamus
duo		overturned Barbillus' boat
trēs		people fell with Barbillus into the water
Quīntus		surrounded the people in the water
servus		people died
crocodīlī		wounded Barbillus
Aethiopes		helped to save Barbillus

3 When the day ended, what do you think would have been the final
   thoughts of

   a Quintus

   b the astrologer

   c Barbillus?

   If you are in a group, divide these characters between you. When you have
   finished, compare their final thoughts.

Check

Practising the language p. 125

Ex. 1 This practises the use of **hic** and **ille** and
        is based on the story of the crocodile hunt.
        Write out the sentences as instructed.

Ex. 2 This exercise is quite difficult and you may like to work with a partner. Do
        examples **a–f** as instructed and then check your answers. If you have got them
        all right or made only one mistake, you need only write down the required Latin
        word in the remaining examples. Otherwise write out the rest of the examples
        as before.

Check

About the language 2: imperatives p. 121

Para. 1 This contains examples of the *imperative* forms of the verbs **spectāre** and **venīre**.
         An imperative is used when giving an *order* to someone. Note the difference
         between the singular and plural forms.

Para. 2 Look carefully at the forms in the table and note the similarity between the
         imperative and *infinitive* forms of each verb, e.g. **portā**, **portāte**, **portāre**.

         Now write out the other Latin verb forms in paragraph 2 in the same way. As
         with **portāre**, underline the corresponding letters. Are there any exceptions to
         the pattern?

Para. 3 This tells you the way in which people are ordered not to do things. Read the
         examples and explanation and notice the difference between singular and plural
         forms.

Para. 4 Without writing them down, work out the examples as instructed.

Further examples Using paragraph 2 as a guide, write down

        1 the *imperative singular* of: **aedificāre**; **pūnīre**; **claudere**;

        2 the *imperative plural* of: **dēlēre**; **līberāre**; **mittere**.

Check

The Nile

The Nile was a popular subject for mosaics and wall-paintings. See examples on pp. 123, 124, 127 and 147.

The Nile hunting scene below is based on a mosaic.

Label the picture using the Latin words in the box below.

flōs	aqua	fēlēs	āra	serpēns	rīpa
scapha	templum	palūs	casa	crocodīlus	saxum
īnsula	hasta	hippopotamus			

 Check

About the language 3: vocative case p. 124

Para. 1   This explains the use of the vocative case.

Paras. 2–4   Read and then translate all the examples.

Further exercises   1   Look again at the vocative singular forms in paragraph 3. Write down:

     a   the vocative singular of: **Quīntus; dominus; vēnālīcius; Caecilius;**

     b   the vocative singular of: **gladiātor; ancilla; puer;**

     c   the vocative plural of: **rēx; nauta; servus.**

   2   The vocative is often found in sentences which contain a verb in the imperative form. From paragraphs 1, 3 and 4, write down the Latin sentences which contain an imperative (there are FOUR sentences altogether).

 Check

Vocabulary checklist 19 p. 130

Learn the words as far as **illūc** and answer the questions.

1 Which of these characters could be described as *amorous*?

2 What do these verb forms mean: **cōnfēcerat; comparāre; cōgitāte**?

3 Why is a rich person sometimes described as *affluent*? What is meant by describing a situation as being 'in a state of *flux'*?

4 What is the connection between the English word *fortuitous* and the Latin **forte**?

5 What are you doing when you show your *gratitude* to someone?

Learn the rest of the words.

6 When would you find an *itinerary* useful?

7 Why could your headteacher be described as acting *in locō parentis*? When is a doctor referred to as a *locum*?

8 In Italy you sometimes see a warning *pericolo di morte*. Why should you keep away?

9 What kind of a person is a *vivacious* one?

10 The new building provoked much *vociferous* opposition. What does this mean?

Check

Language test

1 Complete the sentences by ticking the correct word.

a _____ puerī pecūniam quaerēbant. (illī, illōs)

b ego _____ fābulam nārrāvī. (haec, hanc)

c _____ āra prō templō erat. (haec, hae)

d dux _____ mīlitēs laudāvit. (hunc, hōs)

e _____ crocodīlus servum interfēcit. (hic, hoc)

f _____ monumentum antīquum erat. (ille, illud)

2 Complete the sentences and then translate them.

a serve, _____ hastam! (tenē, tenēte)

b _____ celeriter ex urbe, Clēmēns! (fuge, fugite)

c nōlī latrōnibus _____ , mercātor! (resiste, resistere)

d puellae, _____ pugnāre in viā! (nōlī, nōlīte)

e _____ statim ad portum! (festīnāre, festīnāte)

3 Translate the sentences.

    a frāter, pompam vix vidēre potes.

    b tabernārī, hunc librum emere volō.

    c cūr tot vīllās habēs, Barbille?

    d meī amīcī, multum vīnum poscite!

    e fīlia, amā mātrem patremque!

 Check

Revision

Nouns pp. 150–2

You have now learnt all the cases of the noun except one which you will meet in Book III.

First study the table on p. 150. The first and second declension nouns **puella** and **servus** will already be familiar to you. **puer** and **templum** are now added to the table. As you will see, the endings of **puer** and **templum** are the same as those of **servus** except in the nominative and vocative singular. **templum** is also different from **servus** because it is a neuter noun.

In the table on p. 151 you are given the third declension nouns **cīvis**, **rēx**, **urbs** and **nōmen** in addition to the familiar **mercātor** and **leō**. As you already know, the endings of the nominative (and vocative) singular of third declension nouns vary considerably, but the other endings are the same. There is one exception: the neuter noun **nōmen** does not change in the accusative. (This is true of all neuter nouns – compare **templum**.)

Exercise As a quick revision of the use of the different cases translate the following sentences and give the case of the nouns in **bold type**.

	Latin	English	Case
1	**leō** in silvā ambulābat; lacrimābat quod pēs dolēbat.		
2	in pede **leōnis** erat spīna.		
3	pāstor **leōnem** vīdit.		
4	'ō **leō**, quam miser es!' inquit.		
5	pāstor **leōnī** celeriter auxilium dedit; spīnam extrāxit.		

Paras. 1–4	Learn by heart **puella**, **servus** and **mercātor**. You will then be able to recognise quickly the case endings of most nouns in the three declensions.
Para. 5	Cover up the noun tables and see if you can do the sentences without looking at the table.
Para. 6	Write out this exercise, noticing especially whether the nouns are singular or plural.
Para. 7	This paragraph revises the genitive case. Do the examples in your head, then write down the Latin words in each sentence which are in the genitive case and whether they are singular or plural.

Genitives		Singular/plural
a		
b		
c		
d		
e		
f		

Para. 8	Without looking at the tables on pp. 150–1, do this exercise as instructed.

Case		Singular/plural
a		
b		
c		
d		
e		
f		
g		
h		

Check

Vocabulary p. 170

Read the notes in paragraph 1 and do the examples in paragraphs 2, 3 and 4. Can you do the examples in paragraph 4 without looking at the noun tables?

Check

Para. 5	Read.

Adjectives p. 153

Paras. 1–3 Read and learn the endings of **bonus** and **fortis**. This will be easy if you have already learnt the noun endings of the three declensions.

Para. 4 Do the exercise as instructed.
Check

Verbs with the dative p. 164

Read paragraphs 1 and 2 and translate the further examples in paragraph 3.

Further exercise Translate the following sentences.

1 latrōnēs senī obstābant.

2 omnēs mihi cōnfīdēbant.

3 servus mē fortiter dēfendēbat.

4 Eutychus fēlī sacrae resistere nōn poterat.

5 magna multitūdō viās urbis complēbat.

Which sentences contain a verb which is used with the dative case?
Check

Progress record

Textbook pp. 111–30   Student Study Book pp. 67–80

Stage 19 Īsis	Done	Revised	Any problems?
The worship of Isis			
Model sentences			
Aristō			
diēs fēstus I			
diēs fēstus II			
pompa			
About the language 1: **hic** and **ille**			
The worship of Isis continued			
vēnātiō I			
vēnātiō II			
Practising the language			
About the language 2: imperatives			
The Nile			
About the language 3: vocative case			
Vocabulary checklist 19			
Language test			
Revision			

Stage 20 medicus

In this Stage you find out what happened to Barbillus after he was wounded in the crocodile hunt. You meet Petro, a Greek doctor, and learn about different methods of treating patients in the Roman world.

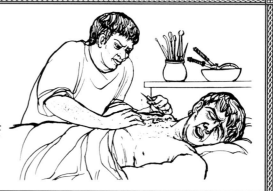

Picture p. 131

This is a seal stone, greatly enlarged. On the right, a doctor examines the swollen stomach of a young man. On the left, Asclepius, the god of medicine, leans on his staff, around which a serpent is coiled. (The staff with its serpent, the **caduceus**, is still used as a symbol of the medical profession.)

Model sentences p. 132

Read the sentences, using the pictures to guide you to the meaning. Now see if you can answer the following questions by filling in the right word. There is one question for each model sentence.

Sentence 1 What are the slaves described as doing when they returned to the villa? _____ Barbillus.

Sentence 2 What were the slave-girls doing as they stood near the bed?
_____

Sentence 3 What was the astrologer doing as he broke into the bedroom?
_____

Sentence 4 What was Barbillus doing when he heard the astrologer? _____ in bed.

Sentence 5 What was Phormio doing when he hurried to the city? _____ a doctor.

Check

Astrology

You will have noticed that the astrologer who warned Barbillus not to go hunting has appeared again in this Stage. He was a member of Barbillus' household whose job was to advise him about decisions he had to make.

Astrologers believe that the movement of the planets and the twelve constellations of the zodiac have an effect on human life; they claim that if they know the time and date of a person's birth they will be able to predict what the future may hold.

Astrologers are still popular today as is shown by the horoscopes in newspapers and magazines. There is no scientific evidence to support them.

lūna Scorpiōnem intrat. What does this mean?
Check

remedium astrologī p. 133

In this story two people treat Barbillus: Phormio and the astrologer. If you are in a group half of you could answer the questions about Phormio and half those about the astrologer. Check the answers and then tell the other group what your character did. Everyone should answer questions 1 and 16.

Introduction (lines 1–2)

1   Why is the situation so urgent? Which TWO Latin words in line 1 show this urgency?

Phormio (lines 2–15)

2   Phormio is an experienced First Aider. How has he gained his experience (lines 2–3)?

3   What had he done when Barbillus was injured?

4   Why was it unsuccessful?

5   Why do you think Phormio sent the slave-girls out of the bedroom (line 8)?

6   Give the line numbers to which this picture refers.

7   Why did Phormio want these (line 11)?

8   What did he do with them when they arrived?

The astrologer (lines 16–28)

9   Why did the astrologer burst into the bedroom (lines 16–17)?

10   Translate and fill in what the astrologer said (line 18).

11   Who would you connect to this balloon?   Do you have a cure?

12   The astrologer is confident that he can cure Barbillus. How does he show this in lines 20–1? Give two examples of his confidence.

13   What is the astrologer going to do with this?

14   When Barbillus heard the astrologer's intention, what did he ask Quintus to do (line 28)?

15   Why do you think Barbillus whispered?

For everyone (lines 29–30)

16 The last two sentences are quite difficult. Translate them, paying special attention to cases and verb endings.

Spiders' webs and a dead mouse were used to treat Barbillus' wound.

Choose nouns and verbs from the story to fill in the spaces in the web and on the mouse. The cases and tenses are shown at the centre of the web and on the mouse. You will be able to find examples for every space except one. If you are in a group, you could compare your answers.

Check

Petrō p. 134

Petro now arrives at Barbillus' villa in response to Phormio's summons.
Read lines 1–6.

1 Why was Petro furious with the astrologer?

2 How did he show his anger?

Read lines 7–19.

3 Having got rid of the astrologer, Petro set about treating Barbillus' wound. Pictured below are the things he used. As you read through the story, write down what Petro did with each of them.

(lines 7–8)

 _____

_____

(lines 14–17)

 _____

_____

(lines 17–18)

 _____

_____

(lines 18–19)

 _____

_____

4 Why was Petro worried about Barbillus' condition (lines 11–13)?

Read lines 20 to the end.

5 What advice did Petro give Quintus about Barbillus' treatment (lines 20–3)?

6 Write out a translation of the last paragraph.

Check

Medical instruments

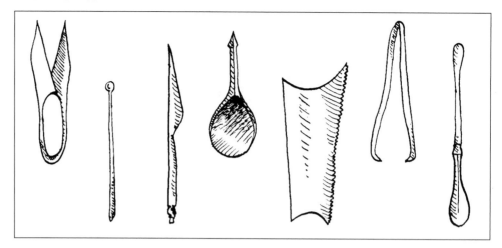

These medical instruments were used in Roman times.

Put the correct number next to the items in the picture by using the following names and descriptions.

1 *forceps*: for extracting objects from wounds, etc.;

2 *saw*: for amputating limbs;

3 *combined probe and spatula*: for exploring wounds, etc.; the spatula was used for spreading ointments;

4 *ligula*: a small scoop for extracting medicine and ointments from narrow-necked bottles;

5 *shears*: used mainly for cutting hair;

6 *scalpel*: a knife used in operations;

7 *tongue depressor*: for holding down the tongue.

Check

About the language 1: present participles p. 135

Para. 1 Read.

Para. 2 Translate the examples. Then pick out the Latin participle and noun in each sentence as instructed and complete the table below.

	Participle	Noun
a		
b		
c		
d		

Para. 3 Study the table.

Para. 4 Translate the examples in your head. As instructed, find the present participle and the matching noun in each sentence; then complete the table below.

	Participle	Noun	Case	Singular or plural
a				
b				
c				
d				
e				

Check

Medicine and science pp. 142–5

Read this section and study the pictures.

Pictures pp. 143–4

After your work on medical instruments on p. 86 of this book, you will be able to recognise some of the instruments in the pictures. On the left of the picture on p. 144 you can see two cases for instruments and a palette for grinding medicines.

1 Look at the pictures of patients below. As a doctor in Alexandria, how would you treat them? Base your remedies on what you have read in the stories as well as in the background section.

a    b    c

2 Eratosthenes, besides calculating the circumference of the Earth, also invented a way of finding all the prime numbers up to a certain size. A prime number is a number that will only divide exactly by itself and 1. For example, 2, 3, 5 and 7 are prime numbers.

a Try Eratosthenes' method to find all the prime numbers up to 100. Look at the square of numbers below. Cross out 1 which is not considered as a prime number. Then cross out all the numbers which are multiples of 2, i.e. 4, 6, 8 etc. Then cross out all the numbers which are multiples of 3, i.e. 6, 9, 12 etc. Do the same with 4, 5, 6, 7, 8, 9 and 10. The numbers which are left will be prime numbers.

1	2	3	4	5	6	7	8	9	10
11	12	13	14	15	16	17	18	19	20
21	22	23	24	25	26	27	28	29	30
31	32	33	34	35	36	37	38	39	40
41	42	43	44	45	46	47	48	49	50
51	52	53	54	55	56	57	58	59	60
61	62	63	64	65	66	67	68	69	70
71	72	73	74	75	76	77	78	79	80
81	82	83	84	85	86	87	88	89	90
91	92	93	94	95	96	97	98	99	100

b What do you notice about the prime numbers?

Check

fortūna crūdēlis pp. 136–7

In this story you learn about the life of Barbillus, his wife Plotina and his son Rufus.

If you are in a group, you could divide up the characters between you; then answer the questions on this and the next page about the character you have chosen and compare answers. Alternatively, you could answer the comprehension questions in your textbook, p. 137.

Barbillus

1 How would you describe your wife (lines 1–2)?

2 How would you describe your son (lines 3–6)?

3 How did you get on with your son's friend Eupor (line 9)?

4 What did you feel about the wedding invitation (lines 12–13)?

5 What advice did your astrologer give and what did you and your wife think of it (lines 16–19)?

6 What made your wife change her mind (lines 19–23)?

7 What decision did you make (line 24)?

8 What tragedy befell your wife (lines 26–8)?

9 How did this affect your relationship with your son (lines 29–30)?

10 Where is he now and what is he doing (lines 32–3)?

Plotina

1 What sort of person were you (lines 1–2)?

2 How would you describe your son (lines 3–6)?

3 How did you get on with your son's friend Eupor (line 9)?

4 When you received Eupor's invitation, what advice did the astrologer give you and your family (lines 16–17)?

5 What did you think of the astrologer's advice (lines 18–19)?

6 How did Rufus get you to change your mind (lines 19–23)?

7 What did your husband decide (line 24)?

8 How far did you get on your journey (lines 26–7)?

9 What was the last thing you saw (lines 27–8)?

10 What thoughts rushed through your mind at that moment?

Rufus

1 What are your interests (lines 3–4)?

2 How did you get on with your parents (lines 5–6)?

3 What plans did your friend Eupor make about his career (lines 7–10)?

4 What did you feel about the invitation to his wedding (lines 10–12)?

5 Why was the astrologer asked for his advice (lines 12–14)?

6 How did the astrologer's advice result in a disagreement with your parents (lines 14–19)?

7 How did you get round your mother (lines 19–23)?

8 What happened on the journey (lines 26–8)?

9 Why didn't you go home (lines 29–30)?

10 What did you do instead (lines 31–3)?

Questions p. 137

Read lines 1–17 and answer questions 1–7.
Read lines 18 to the end and answer the rest of the questions.

Further work

1 From lines 1–10 write down:

   a TWO noun and adjective pairs. Give the case and gender of each of them.

   b ONE genitive singular.

   c ONE pluperfect tense and its meaning.

   d ONE relative clause.

2 From lines 18–24 write down:

   a TWO adjectives in the superlative.

   b TWO verbs which are used with the dative.

   c TWO infinitives.

   d present participle.

Check

Picture p. 137

The ship is driven by oars as well as the wind. The figure of a dolphin decorates the prow on the left. Streamers are hung on the mast and above the helmsman's reed cabin at the stern to indicate the direction of the wind. The ship has eyes, either to see the way or to ward off the evil eye. Eyes can still be seen on many Mediterranean boats today. Compare the ship on p. 137 with the similar one in the drawing below.

About the language 2: *eum, eam*, etc. p. 138

Para. 1   Read the examples and then study the table.

> The masculine and feminine forms are the same in the genitive singular and in the dative singular and plural.

Para. 2   Translate the further examples. Learn the table at the top of p. 138 and then cover it up. Now look at all the Latin sentences in paragraphs 1 and 2. Fill in the table below by picking out the pronouns (**eum**, **eōs**, etc.) in the sentences. You will find there will be some blank spaces in the table.

	Singular			Plural		
	Accusative	Genitive	Dative	Accusative	Genitive	Dative
Masculine						
Feminine						

Check

astrologus victor I pp. 138–9

This story describes the rivalry between the astrologer and Petro, the doctor.

Read lines 1–6 (**Alexandriā**). After you have read these lines, show the differences between the two characters by filling in the table below.

	Astrologer	Petro
Personal qualities		
Nationality		
Place of residence		

Read the Latin lines 6 to the end with the help of the translation below. When you come to the conversation, write a translation in the box.

It was easy therefore for the astrologer to visit Barbillus. He would often come to the bedroom, in which the master was lying ill. When Petro was absent, the astrologer would speak into his master's ear.

Barbillus listened to the astrologer anxiously. But, although the pain grew worse daily, he still trusted the doctor. When Barbillus refused to throw out the doctor, the astrologer had an idea.

astrologus victor II p. 139

As in Part I, read the Latin in lines 1–18 with the translation and write the conversations in the boxes.

The next day the astrologer burst into the master's bedroom, shouting:

When Barbillus heard this, he gave himself over totally to the astrologer. Therefore, after he mixed the ointment, he opened his master's shoulder and smeared it (with the ointment). But the astrologer's ointment was very bad. Barbillus' wound kept growing worse.

When the astrologer noticed this, he ran away from the house in terror. Barbillus,
despairing of his life, summoned me to his bedroom. Whispering in my ear he said,

Read lines 19 to the end, and then answer these questions.

1 At the end of the story Barbillus is described as **obstinātus**. Why do you think he had this attitude?

2 Who finally took charge of the situation?

Check

Picture p. 139

The letter says: Prokleios to his good friend Pekysis greetings. You will do well if, at your own risk, you sell to my friend Sotas such high-quality goods as he will tell you he needs, for him to bring to me at Alexandria. Know that you will have to deal with me about the cost. Greet all your family from me. Farewell.

Practising the language pp. 140–1

Ex. 1 Before doing this exercise, study again the forms of the present participles on p. 135. Then complete the exercises as instructed.

Ex. 2 This exercise gives further practice with the imperative. If you need to revise the imperative forms, look at them again on p. 160. Then work out the sentences as instructed.

Ex. 3 Translate this dialogue in your head. If you can work in pairs one of you could take the part of Aristo and the other Galatea.

As instructed, write out the relative clauses and state the noun which each relative clause describes.

Check

Picture p. 141

Mummy portrait of a young man. Because he is shown naked (unlike the people on pp. 115–17), he is likely to have been a keen athlete used to training in a Greek gymnasium.

Vocabulary checklist 20 p. 146

Learn the checklist as far as **vulnus** and answer these questions:

1 Do you think it is better to be *artful* or *artistic*? Why?

2 *Doctors* should be **doctī**. What does this mean?

3 If you were asked where you were *domiciled*, what would you say?

4 **līberō, liber, lībertus**. Which is the odd one out? Explain.

5 What is the connection between *lunatic* and **lūna**?

6 What is a *post-mortem*?

7 Why would you visit an *oculist*?

8 What is the difference between a *pessimist* and an *optimist*?

9 'He had to *relinquish* all claim to the money.' What does this mean?

10 The Greek hero Achilles was said to be *invulnerable* except for his heel. What was special about his heel?

Now learn the numbers.

1 Give the answers to these sums in Latin:

   a duo + quattuor =

   b ūnus + septem =

   c decem + trīgintā =

   d octō − trēs =

   e trīgintā − vīgintī =

   f novem − trēs =

2 Can you write down the Latin words for the following Roman numerals?

III V VIII XX L IV IX XL VI

Language test

1 Complete the sentences by choosing the correct participle from the box below. Each participle should be used only once. Then translate the sentences.

Singular	Plural
stāns	stantēs
clāmāns	clāmantēs
lacrimāns	lacrimantēs
quaerēns	quaerentēs

   a Barbillus, _____, Quīntō dē morte uxōris nārrāvit.

   b ancillae lectum dominī circumveniēbant, _____.

   c servī ad urbem ruērunt, medicum _____.

   d astrologus ē cubiculō contendit, mūrem _____.

   e Galatēa, _____, iuvenēs adiit.

f iuvenēs, prope Helenam _____, eam avidē spectābant.

g puer Aegyptius, in casā _____, latrōnibus fortiter restitit.

h latrōnēs, _____, puerum superāvērunt.

2 Use the words in the pool below to translate the words in **bold type** in the following story.

eās	eī	eam	eius
eīs	eōs	eum	eōrum

a Aristo was not a happy man. Galatea was always nagging **him** (   ).

b **His** (   ) daughter Helena often invited a lot of young poets to the house.

c They recited rude poems **to her** (   ) and frequently fought with one another.

d Aristo disliked **them** (   ) because he wanted a quiet life.

e In the end he could not stand **their** (   ) bad behaviour any longer.

f He said **to them** (   ) that they must leave the house.

g Helena burst into tears and Galatea tried to comfort **her** (   ).

h Aristo was in despair. 'What have I done', he said, 'to deserve such a wife and daughter? Nothing I do can silence **them** (   ).'

Check

Revision

Comparatives and superlatives pp. 154–5

Paras. 1–4 Study these paragraphs.

- The comparative and superlative forms are based on the accusative of the ordinary adjective (the ordinary forms are explained on the previous page).

- Adjectives like **pulcher** have a different superlative from that of other adjectives.

When you have studied paragraph 3 learn the nominative forms in the table, e.g. **longus, longior, longissimus**.

Now cover up the table and write down the comparatives and superlatives of the adjectives in the box below. The last two adjectives are different from those in the table, but they should not cause you problems.

Ordinary	Comparative	Superlative
cārus		
dulcis		
sacer acc: sacrum		
fēlīx (*lucky*) acc: fēlīcem		
ingēns acc: ingentem		

Paras. 5 and 6 When you have studied the irregular forms in the table, learn them by heart. They are very common. Then translate the further examples in paragraph 6 without looking at the table.

Para. 7 Do the exercise as instructed.

Remember that the superlative, like the ordinary adjective, agrees with the noun it describes.

Para. 8 Do the examples as instructed, taking particular care with the last one.

Pronouns II: *hic, ille, eum*; Pronouns III: *quī* pp. 158–9

Study the tables and the examples on these pages to the end of paragraph 1 on p. 159.

Now close your book and write down the case, number and gender of the pronoun in **bold type** in the sentences below.

Page	Sentence	Case	Number	Gender
158	**hae** stolae sunt sordidae!			
	hunc servum pūnīre volō.			
	illa taberna nunc est mea.			
	spectā **illōs** hominēs!			
	iuvenēs **eam** laudāvērunt.			
	dominus **eī** praemium dedit.			
	ego ad vīllam **eius** contendī.			
	senex **eīs** crēdere nōluit.			
	ille tamen nōn erat perterritus.			
	nēmō **illam** in urbe vīdit.			
159	ursa, **quam** Quīntus vulnerāvit, nunc mortua est.			
	ubi est templum, **quod** Augustus Caesar aedificāvit?			
	in mediō ātriō stābant mīlitēs, **quī** rēgem custōdiēbant.			

Para. 2 Work out the sentences in your head and write down the antecedent and relative pronoun.

Para. 3 Write out a translation of the sentences.

Longer sentences II p. 169

Para. 1 Study the sentences.

Para. 2 Translate the examples in your head.

In the Latin sentences in paragraphs 1 and 2, a word has been left out in the second part of the sentences because it is really a repetition from the first part, e.g. **Rēgnēnsēs erant laetī, Canticī (erant) miserī.**

Sometimes the form of the missing word would have to be changed to fit in with the meaning, e.g. **ūnus servus est fūr, cēterī (sunt) innocentēs. cēterī** is a plural word and so **sunt** must be supplied instead of **est**.

Write down the word missing from the second sentence in paragraphs 1 and 2.

Para. 3 Study the examples. In these sentences a word has been left out in the first part, but appears in the second part, e.g. **sacerdōs templum (quaerēbat), poēta tabernam quaerēbat.**

Write down the word missing from the second sentence in this paragraph.

Para. 4 Translate the further examples. Write down the word missing from sentences **c** and **d**.

Check

Progress record

Stage 20 medicus	Done	Revised	Any problems?
Model sentences			
Astrology			
remedium astrologī			
Petrō			
Medical instruments			
About the language 1: present participles			
Medicine and science			
fortūna crūdēlis			
About the language 2: **eum**, **eam**, etc.			
astrologus victor I			
astrologus victor II			
Practising the language			
Vocabulary checklist 20			
Language test			
Revision			

Short guide to the pronunciation of Latin

short vowels

a   as in English 'aha'

e   as in English 'pet'

i   as in English 'dip'

o   as in English 'pot'

u   as in English 'put'

y   as in French 'plume'

long vowels (marked as follows)

ā   as in English 'father'

ē   as in French 'fiancée'

ī   as in English 'deep'

ō   as in French 'beau' (roughly as in English 'coat')

ū   as in English 'fool' (not as in 'music')

diphthongs (two vowels sounded together in a single syllable)

ae   as in English 'high'

au   as in English 'how'

ei   as in English 'day'

eu   no exact English equivalent: 'e' is combined with 'oo' (not as in 'few')

oe   as in English 'boy'

ui   no exact English equivalent: 'u' is combined with 'i'

consonants

b   (usually) as in English 'big'

b   (followed by t or s) as in English 'lips'

c   as in English 'cat' or 'king' (not as in 'centre' or 'cello')

ch   as in English 'cat' pronounced with emphasis (not as in 'chin')

g   as in English 'got' (not as in 'gentle')

gn   as 'ngn' in English 'hangnail'

i   (before a vowel and sometimes written as j) as in English 'you'

n   (usually) as in English 'net'

n   (before c, g or qu) as in English 'anger'

ph   as in English 'pig' pronounced with emphasis (not as in 'photo')

qu   as in English 'quick'

r   as Scottish ('rolled') r in 'bird'

s   as in English 'sing' (not as in 'roses')

th   as in English 'terrible' pronounced with emphasis (not as in 'the' or 'theatre')

v   (often written as u) as in English 'wind'

x   as in English 'box'

Other consonants are pronounced as in English.

double consonants

ll   as in English 'hall-light' (not as in 'taller')

nn   as in English 'thin-nosed' (not as in 'dinner')

pp   as in English 'hip-pocket' (not as in 'happy')

Word stress (indicated in this section by *italic type*)

In spoken Latin a syllable in each word is stressed. The following are the general rules for deciding where the stress should fall:

1   In a word of two syllables, the stress is on the first syllable, e.g. m*ā*ter, c*o*quus.

2   In a word of more than two syllables,

   a) the stress falls on the second syllable from the end if that syllable contains a long vowel, or a short vowel followed by two consonants, e.g. sal*ū*tat, Met*e*lla;

   b) otherwise the stress falls on the third syllable from the end, e.g. Caec*i*lius, f*u*rcifer, laet*i*ssimus.

Further examples (with stress marked)

am*ī*cus	s*e*det	v*ī*lla
p*ā*vō	l*a*etus	l*au*dat
qu*o*que	lab*ō*rat	m*a*gnus
i*ā*nua	*ē*heu	v*ī*num
v*e*rberat	qu*a*erit	*ū*nus